AMERICA'S WILDLIFE SAMPLER

Library of Congress CIP Data: page 207

AMERICA'S
WILDLIFE
SAMPLER

CELEBRATING AMERICA

You round a turn on a wooded path and there's a doe drinking at the edge of the lake. Heart racing, you gingerly put down the other boot and unintentionally snap a twig. The frightened doe stiffens at the sound—head bolts up, ears perk, nostrils sniff the wind. She knows you are there. Tail flags, hoofs fly, and off she bounds into the forest of balsam fir. It's all over in a matter of seconds, but what a precious few seconds to remember.

Moments such as these are special to all of us who value wildlife and the out-of-doors. So special, we think, that we have devoted this book to similar vignettes from every region in the country. Turn the pages of *America's Wildlife Sampler* and you'll probably recognize many of the scenes because most of our "samplings" are typical, common sights from your part of America, be it Maine or Hawaii.

Depending upon where you live, your own experience might not include seeing a deer at a lake in the woods. Instead, you may have glimpsed a fox prowling around a Midwest farmyard or a flock of terns coming down on your hometown Florida beach. Or perhaps it is the changing seasons in New England that are the strongest in your memory. Those moments when you can faintly see fall's subtle beginnings in the first show of color in a tree along your street, or in dazzling sunbeams on a clear, crisp September afternoon.

It may be the hollow flutelike sound of a wood thrush in a Southern garden or the sudden blossoming of desert flowers that you remember best. Or wandering through West Coast fog and hearing crying gulls dipping into the sea.

Some pages of our book will be a homecoming for you; others will be a journey of exploration and discovery. Each and every page, though, will remind you of the beauty of the country you call home. Our writers and photographers made sure of that. Their words and pictures make each chapter seem like a celebration with a medley of moods and images that evoke the very spirit of America the beautiful.

At the end of each chapter, we have included regional almanacs filled with recipes, weather wisdom, wildlife notes, humor—a homespun collection of good things for you to read.

For the staff, working on this book has been immensely satisfying. Imagine—a chance to steep ourselves in the distinctive wildlife and landscapes of every region of the country—from the rolling green hills of the East across plains, alpine meadows, rocky peaks, deserts, coastal cliffs and tundra to our tropical island state in the middle of the Pacific Ocean.

Above all, we took particular pleasure in knowing that there would be a little bit of each one of your lives somewhere within the covers. We hope that these pages will help you to relive some of the special moments you have enjoyed in nature and will reveal unfamiliar places to you so clearly that you will feel as though you have already been there.

Your editor,

Barbara Peters

THE NORTHEAST

by REEVE L. BROWN

The land was ours before we were the land's
She was our land more than a hundred years
Before we were her people . . .

Robert Frost, "The Gift Outright"

The Northeast, even more than a region, is an enduring image. Its landscape and its history lie at the back of the American mind the way the scenery of childhood remains the secret homeland of the adult imagination. Americans who have spent all their lives in Iowa or California, Texas or Hawaii, often still feel a kind of possessiveness about the vision of a country village "back East." White houses and red barns, sharp-spired churches, surrounding forests that may contain trees already standing at the time of the Revolution or cross-stitched miles of old stone walls built by the early settlers who cleared the land for farmsteads.

There persists even today, in this part of the world, an old respect for the hard-won equilibrium between the earth and those who would make their living from it, as well as a lingering pioneer's sense of the natural world as an ambiguous presence: half challenge, half wonder. There is evidence, too, of an abiding tradition of guardianship, passed down from generation to generation, as if the inhabitants here take seriously their role as custodians of the national memory, with its legacy of farm and forest and the necessary daily awareness of living creatures, both domestic and wild.

The uncommon man who harvests a Christmas tree from his own woods and brings it home on a horse-drawn sled with his grandson beside him may plant a maple in the spring. The sapling may stand in his dooryard in a row of maples that was set out by his own grandfather.

They're bringing home the tree for Christmas.
(Overleaf) The quaint village of Waits River,
Vermont, alive in full fall color.

During the quiet trip across December fields, the boy may spot the tracks of a red fox crossing the trail just in front of the team of Belgian horses. Or the sled may come upon a young deer browsing at the edge of the snow-covered meadow, unaware of their approach. Grandfather reins in the horses quickly and whispers a warning to the child: "Hush! Take care! This moment is too rare to spoil!" And though the man may have venison in the freezer from the fall, and though he and the boy look forward to hunting next year, there is still reverence in their watching.

10

A red fox or a white-tailed deer
could be just a stone's throw from
this New England barn.

The Belgians stamp restlessly, the deer starts, vanishes, and the sled moves on. It traverses a landscape that offers other glimpses of nature arrested and off-guard, with familiar objects frozen into an out-of-season grace: a single stalk of Queen Anne's lace, its blossom stripped and ice-shaped to become a skeleton tulip; a vacant bird's nest, dignified by frost. Overhead, the branches of the hardwoods are burdened, whitened, thickened into antlers; and in the brook that parallels the path, a shallow ripple has been caught 'til spring in a paradox of rigid motion.

Winter whitens a country churchyard and frosts a warbler's nest and a stalk of Queen Anne's lace.

A white-throated sparrow fluffs its feathers against the cold as twilight shadows cross a snowy farm field.

The air is still and very cold. The horses move faster, heading toward the animal heat of the barn, the warmth of the wood-burning stove in the farmhouse kitchen.

A northeastern winter can be an isolating experience. Each farm stays busy with daily chores that accompany the cold. The furnace and the stoves must be tended constantly, the animals and the family must be fed regularly and well. Now birds gather at the feeders, for severe weather keenly diminishes their food sources. Our neighbor calls these winter birds his

"chickens" and feeds them as conscientiously as he does his hens.

Though the days are short and the snow is deep, outdoor activities balance indoor work. Some people strap on snowshoes and walk in the woods looking for wildlife. For others, snow-mobiles and cross-country skis have made the winter landscape more accessible than ever before. Ice-fishing huts dot deep-frozen lakes, and on ponds and lakes kept free of snow, skaters' patterns score the ice while below, near the muddy bottom, bass and pickerel wait for the thaw.

In early evening, silhouettes of passing Canada geese give a moment's magic to skaters on Lake Champlain.

16

When spring finally does come, it comes like a liberating army, accompanied on all sides by freedom's clamorous ring: the wild honking of Canada geese on their way to northern breeding grounds again, the yipping of foxes calling to each other, the hammering of a pileated woodpecker, the excited chattering of chipmunks and the *chir-r-r-r, chir-r-r-r* of the red squirrel, the headlong rush and tumble of rivers and streams flood-high with melted snow, and in some hardwood forests, the steady drip of sap into thousands of buckets at maple sugaring time.

Maple sugar time—when buckets of sap boil down into a delectable sweet.

Sugaring is an annual ritual that depends upon the tug-of-war between winter's departure and spring's arrival, those few interim weeks when warm days are followed by cold nights. The sap begins to flow, but the leaf buds do not yet start to swell. Although commercial maple sugar producers rely on networks of tubing to drain all the trees in one area, some farmers in the far north still collect sap in the traditional buckets, then pour the contents of these into a gathering tank to be hauled by tractor or horses to the sugarhouse, where the sap is boiled down to syrup.

The sugarhouse spews forth smoke and steam like some giant outdoor pressure cooker, and the sweet-scented mist fills the air with a prophesy everyone can smell and taste: the heady promise of spring.

Sensing the coming season, sparrow hawks perch on the fenceposts around newly bare pastures, waiting for insects to emerge from the awakening earth, while the screams of angry crows tell that the great horned owl is abroad, hunting for rodents, rabbits, or even skunks with which to feed a growing family. These owls nest and hatch out their young earlier in the season than most birds do. My husband saw a trio of owlets in late February. They were looking out of their nest in the crotch of a beech tree, each of them wearing a comical skullcap of snow.

Throughout the northeastern states, whether it be the obstinate, granite-studded land of New England's hill farms or the rich soil of the great agricultural regions of New York and Pennsylvania, the turning of the earth marks the turning of the year.

In a willow thicket, a drowsy great horned owl awaits the evening hunt.

Farmers everywhere, sitting on tractors or, rarely, following a couple of horses with a walking plow, take part in the rite of burial and resurrection: plowing under the depleted ground, plowing up the new, life-giving soil and all the creatures it harbors. The farmers will be glad of the company of hungry robins hopping from furrow to furrow searching for insects, which return in force as spring advances. Some, like ladybird beetles, are as welcome as the robins because they live on aphids and other insects that destroy crops.

Ladybird beetles feed on the pollen of dandelions near a field still being plowed the old-fashioned way.

22

An old stone wall borders a pasture
where a cottontail hides in deep clover.

Later in the season, when the grass is high and the fences are mended, the barnyard animals will be turned out to pasture. It is a pleasure to watch them on that very first day as they taste the green feast spread before them and the freedom all around. Heifers that have spent the whole winter in barns now kick up their heels to gallop around the meadow, while young horses stand alert, sniffing the air.

Close by, wild things are busy too. Cotton-tail rabbits nibble on the first patches of clover, woodchucks emerge from their burrows and deer graze at the edges of the pasture, never far from their hidden dappled fawns. All will share with the domestic grazing animals the banquet of

In Maine woods, a lake-side cottage might share a quiet morning with a pair of young bull moose in velvet.

timothy, clover, orchard grass and alfalfa. And deep in the northern swamps and bogs, the moose are browsing on the twigs and bark of saplings or feeding on pondweeds, water lilies and other aquatic plants newly available to them after the long, arid winter.

From the first warm days of spring to the frosty nights of early fall, all of us tend to work our way toward water. We may go to sea in a sailboat, paddle a kayak down the Connecticut River, take a canoe to a quiet lake in Maine, or fish with a fly rod in a nearby stream. The water

Atlantic puffins make their summer home
near a lighthouse off the Maine coast
where the fishing is good.

itself suggests relaxation and retreat, a chance to
get away from the calendar and the clock and to
get closer to nature.

For the people who depend upon the sea
for a living, it is more serious. The history of
the lighthouse keepers of the North Atlantic
coast records two centuries of long hours, raging
storms, and barren isolation broken only by the
cries of the gulls and cormorants or, on Machias
Seal Island and Matinicus Rock, off the coast of
Maine, by the comic relief of clownish colonies
of Atlantic puffins.

Stonington, Maine, is a typical home port for lobstermen like this one pulling a crab from his trap.

Fishing and lobstering communities, too, know the hazards and strains of coastal living. Lobstermen today, facing increased competition and a dwindling lobster supply caused by overharvesting and unwise fishing practices, haul many times more traps and work longer hours than their parents and grandparents did.

The inland harvests of the Northeast have their own difficulties, both climatic and economic, but harvest time here bears a color and an atmosphere unique to the region. The growing season is brief, so that by the time the last cutting of hay is in the barn and the pumpkins, squashes and green tomatoes have been piled in heaps or set out on newspaper to ripen in the cellar, the days are already growing short. Barn swallows that dived and swooped around us during the summer are gone. At night we sometimes hear flocks of geese settle in the stubbed

31

cornfields. Under the beech trees, grouse search among prickly burrs for the succulent nuts. The leaves have begun to turn. Suddenly, the hillsides are no longer soothing billows of summer green, rolling back in gentle invitation to the eye. Instead, fierce reds, oranges, and wild yellows defy the end of the season with a last burst of light before the darker time begins again.

Soon the wildlife retreat to winter quarters. Strong winds send deer toward their yards in the sheltered parts of the forest, squirrels and raccoons to their hollow trees. The woods are

A youngster bringing in the pumpkins probably has his mind on carving jack-o'-lanterns for Halloween.

32

carpeted with ferns and leaves and, in the early
mornings, are chill and enigmatic with autumn.

There is a mist rising from the lakes now
too that adds an air of mystery to the intense,
pervasive quiet, broken only by the canoeist's
gentle paddling or by the flapping of a great blue
heron startled from the marsh grasses.

There is a kind of nostalgia in a northeastern
autumn that is hard to define, a sense of looking
back, of longing. Whether the quality of light at
this time of year causes this feeling, or whether it
is the change in temperature, or in the landscape,
it is hard to be sure. Whatever it is, whatever
it means, Americans throughout the country
should remember—the Northeast was the
beginning; it belongs to all of us. We can
always return.

A lone canoeist enjoys morning on
Chapman Lake in Pennsylvania.
(Overleaf) Pale orange ferns set the
stage for brilliant fall foliage to come.

NORTHEAST

STATES OF THE REGION

Connecticut — *Nutmeg State*
Maine — *Pine Tree State*
Massachusetts — *Bay State*
New Hampshire — *Granite State*
New Jersey — *Garden State*
New York — *Empire State*
Pennsylvania — *Keystone State*
Rhode Island — *Ocean State*
Vermont — *Green Mountain State*

A RARE BIRD

Our national symbol, the bald eagle, appears frequently in folk art on wallpaper, doorways, weather vanes, flagpoles, company logos and samplers. Those are about the *only* places that this noble bird can be seen in most of the country. In the Northeast, where eagle folk art originated, more than two dozen bald eagles could once be spotted easily on a day's ride through the woods. Now there appear to be fewer than eighty breeding pairs in the whole region, with ninety percent of them in Maine.

1800-AND-FROZE-TO-DEATH

On the damp and dreary days of early spring, old-timers often say "I never knew a year when spring didn't come. . . ." But in 1816, spring never did come to New England, and neither did summer. Heavy snows and frosts continued through August. Then, during the winter of 1817, the mercury froze in the thermometers!

What caused that severe cold spell? Volcanic eruptions rocked the Pacific from 1812 to 1817, spewing dense clouds of dust high into the atmosphere. Scientists conjecture that this dust screened out the sun's warming rays, dramatically altering the climate of the entire earth.

WEATHER RHYME AND REASON

"Wild geese, wild geese, going out to sea, all fine weather it will be," say New England lobstermen and fishermen who study weather signs to avoid being caught in storms. They have learned from years of observation that ocean-going birds congregate on beaches instead of flying out to sea when a storm is approaching. Why? Before a storm, air currents flow predominantly downward, making flight difficult.

COUNTING-OUT RHYME

*Silver bark of beech, and sallow
Bark of yellow birch and yellow
    Twig of willow.*

*Stripe of green in moosewood maple
Color seen in leaf of apple,
    Bark of popple.*

*Wood of popple pale as moonbeam,
Wood of oak for yoke,
    and barn-beam,
    Wood of hornbeam.*

*Silver bark of beech, and hollow
Stem of elder, tall and yellow
    Twig of willow.*
            — Edna St. Vincent Millay

A WILDFLOWER FIT FOR A QUEEN

Clusters of gossamer white Queen Anne's lace, their regal heads waving gently in the summer breezes, adorn many New England roadsides and meadows. Legend says they got their name from Queen Anne of England who challenged her ladies-in-waiting to tat a lace as lovely as the wildflowers that bordered the royal garden. When none could rival the Queen's own exquisite handiwork, the flower was named in her honor. A careful look at the flowers reveals the difficulty of the Queen's request, for each three-inch flower head is made up of 75 smaller heads. Each of these smaller heads contains 2,500 tiny perfect flowers, adding up to nearly 200,000 flowers in each white umbrella!

A-HUNTING THEY DID GO

The times have changed! Two hundred years ago, a group of hunters gathered in Pennsylvania to scour the area for game. Within a circle 30 miles across, they bagged 41 cougars, 109 wolves, 112 foxes, 114 bobcats, 17 black bear, 2 elk, 98 deer, 111 buffalo, 3 fishers (large members of the weasel family), 1 otter, 12 wolverines, 3 beavers and nearly 500 smaller animals. Of these, wolves, buffalo and wolverines no longer survive wild in the eastern United States at all, while cougars occur only rarely in remote areas of the South. A few hundred elk have been reintroduced in Pennsylvania and Michigan, and fishers appear only in New England.

CHARGOGOGGAGO, FOR SHORT

Old Indian names for lakes and towns in New England may sound like a mouthful, but they often imparted more information than simple lables like *Long Lake* or *Round Pond.* The original Indian name of a Massachusetts lake, *Chargogoggagomanchaugochaubunagungamaug,* may even have kept peace among neighboring tribes. It meant "You fish on your side of the lake. I fish on my side. Nobody fishes in the middle."

JUST DESSERTS

Maple sugaring is hard work, but you'll appreciate why New Englanders have gone to all that effort for generations if you cook some maple syrup down to the consistency of molasses and serve it warm on vanilla ice cream, lemon sherbet, rice pudding or plain custards.

PUMPKIN SCONES

It doesn't take a large patch to produce more pumpkins than anyone needs for jack-o'-lanterns and Thanksgiving pies. Try your extra pumpkin in these scones, or baking powder biscuits:

1¾ cups sifted all-purpose flour	½ tsp ginger ⅓ cup chilled butter
4 tsp baking powder	½ cup raisins
¾ tsp salt	1 cup sieved cooked pumpkin
¼ cup granulated sugar	melted butter
2 tsp cinnamon	sugar

Preheat oven to 450°. Sift first 6 ingredients together. Cut in butter; mix in raisins. Make a well and add pumpkin; mix lightly, adding a little more pumpkin to make a soft dough. Knead 10 seconds on a lightly floured board. Divide into three portions. Pat each into a 5-inch round and place, well apart, on a greased cookie sheet. Score each round into quarters. Brush with melted butter and sprinkle with sugar. Bake 10 to 15 minutes; serve warm with a cup of tea.

THE SOUTH

by THOMAS B. ALLEN

South means warmth, the gentle force that moves slowly northward, defeating the cold, erasing the snows. South means that part of our country, and that part of us, where winter may come but does not dwell. There may be dark days in a season or in a soul, and in those chill hours, cold may strike an orchard or a heart. Just beyond, though, is the promise of warmth, the promise that travels north each spring.

Our South is too temperate to be always warm. The South knows winter—from the ice shores of Chesapeake Bay and floes dotting the Potomac to the prayerful smudge fires in the frost-threatened groves of Florida. Snow mantles the Great Smoky Mountains that roof the South, and snow whips across the dunes on the islands of the Outer Banks. Cold huddles in the hollows of the Appalachians, where stacks of firewood dwindle around the cabins and the deer come as

boldly as the sparrow in quest of food placed out by people who care.

Winter is short-lived in the South, and by March the land begins to stir in timeless ways. A walk down a country road on an early spring day becomes a journey into the past. The cabin in the flowering woods seems to be a vision from America's earliest days. Yet the split rail fence is not some quaint heirloom; it still works —"horse-high, bull-strong, and pig-tight" as ever. In the gloaming, the soft air bears the first faint scent of apple blossoms and the nocturne of the mockingbird. From such a day comes a feeling of wandering amid a people in a place somehow set apart.

The mountains tell an old story of land and life. In the ice ages, cold moving down the long Appalachian valleys killed native wildlife, and cold-weather species took their place. When the

Blossoming fruit trees herald spring
on the Blue Ridge Parkway, Virginia.
(Overleaf) A South Carolina cabin roof-
deep in azaleas, dogwood and wisteria.

ice retreated, red spruce and fir, red squirrel and water shrew stayed behind. They now live in harmony side-by-side with wildflower and firefly, magnolia and copperhead, and countless other plants and animals that flourish in the nurturing climate of the South.

In the Great Smoky Mountains National Park—that virgin woodland of hemlock and hickory, dogwood and birch, tulip poplar and maple—there are as many varieties of trees as can be found growing in all of Europe and more than 1,400 species of flowering plants.

Round-lobed hepatica nestles in a spring wood near a very different beauty, a coiled copperhead.

This mossy waterfall creates a cool
retreat in the Great Smoky Mountains,
attracting raccoons and black bears in
search of water or food.

Hikers in the park may meet any of a variety
of mammals prowling about the clumps of
mountain laurel or rhododendron. Black bears
are so used to people that the meeting place may
be a garbage can as often as along a forest stream.
Tiny hand-shaped tracks near a picnic table
will give away a marauding raccoon. The track
of the opossum, almost star-shaped, can be the
sign of more than one free-loader if the 'possum
is a mother with seven or eight hungry young on
her back. While resting in the cool refuge of a
shade tree, summer visitors may be startled by the

sudden shrieking of another "camp robber," a raucous blue and white bird calling its name "Jay! Jay!" to scold the trespassers. In the fall, hunters will return the scolding when the squawking jay warns away nearby squirrels. But the hunters can at least thank this inhospitable bird—and the squirrels—for some of the trees around them, produced by the acorns the creatures buried, then neglected to dig up.

Irresponsible hunting, the clearing of deep woods and finally the dying out of chestnut trees that gave it food almost wiped out our biggest

The Virginia opossum may be prowling near a pool where a blue jay pauses to quench its thirst.

upland game bird, the wild turkey. But, thanks
to careful management, it can still be heard,
keow, keow, keow, though seldom seen, as
it struts in open forest or nests in greenbriar.

Hunters in 1912 imported a new game
animal to the South, the European wild boar.
The "Rooshians" later mated with farm pigs
gone wild. Tough descendants—they can kill a
rattlesnake with a stamp of a sharp hoof—roam
the slopes and hollows of the Great Smokies.

The scarlet and the gold have come, and
beyond the woods the trees are in serried rows

In the deep wood, a native turkey struts
his stuff for a mate, while European wild
boars forage in the morning mist.

50

In the Great Smoky Mountains, apples still get pressed in an old cider mill.

and the land has a tamer look. It is fall, and where there had been a scent of apple blossoms there now is a sharper tang. Apple harvest. And something more, a scent so strong it seems to touch the tongue. Cider. The press has been set up, and the apples are tumbling into it. From a worn wooden trough runs a dark amber rivulet. A tin cup appears, and the first cider of the season is tasted and savored.

Out of the mountains now, southwest across piedmont and plain to a place of dark beauty. Here lie the swamps and marshes where Sidney

Lanier, poet laureate of the South, found "the dim sweet woods" and the "braided dusks of the oak and woven shades of the vines." Under live oaks and cypress, a pirogue, that Cajun hybrid of canoe and boat, drifts silently. On a low, bare limb overhanging the somber water, an anhinga perches, its silver-tinged wings outspread to dry. Some call it the snakebird because of its long, sinuous neck and the way it slithers under the water, striking like a snake and skewering fish on its long beak.

In the bayous of Louisiana, levees for flood control keep river water from replenishing the Atchafalaya swamp, imperiling its harmonious community of plants and animals. Bass, crawfish, otter, muskrat, water moccasin, turtle, bullfrog, wood duck, egret, ibis—they all are here, living amid the dredgers. And somewhere in this primeval world may be the last place on earth for the ivory-billed woodpecker, a bird so long unseen that it is feared extinct.

The bald eagle and more than 300 other bird species find refuge in the 1.5 million acres of land and water that are the Florida Everglades. The rarest bird you will see here, if you're

A Louisiana Cajun fishes from his native pirogue, a boat resembling a dugout canoe. (Overleaf) Moss-draped cypress trees are hallmarks of Louisiana's Atchafalaya swamp.

lucky, is the Everglade kite. Wings flapping slowly, head aimed downward, it skims over the tall sawgrass, searching for the only food it will eat—apple snails. Years ago, when developers began disrupting the marsh, animals on less strict diets than the kites managed to survive. Blue herons could eat anything from a fish to a snake. Alligators could hunt farther and harder. But the kites, locked in a restricted predator-prey relationship with the snails, suffered.

When I last saw an Everglade kite, the count was officially 70 to 100. The kite was perched

When an alligator in the Okefenokee swamp guards its nest, birds like this great blue heron keep a respectful distance.

A key deer browses in the Florida Keys
and nutria nap in a Louisiana bayou.

on a dead tree, working on a meal. Through binoculars, I watched the kite pry open the operculum—the snail's trap door. The curvature of the kite's bill corresponded to the curvature of the shell so that the kite was able to slip in its bill and nip the muscle that held the snail's body to the shell. Upon such tiny marvels of adaptive architecture is the intricate realm of the Everglades built.

Like the Everglade kite, the key deer once was near extinction. The tiny deer, about the size of an Irish setter, is found only on the Florida Keys. Protected as an endangered species, the deer now number about 400.

Multiplication went wild for the coypu, better known by the name of its valuable fur, the nutria. Coypus were imported from South America in the 1930's and kept on fur farms in Louisiana. Some escaped and reproduced in

the millions. They now live double lives—as fur-bearers, they are cherished; as foragers in sugar cane fields, they are outlaws.

On the Florida-Georgia border is another small natural world, an immense peat bog the Indians called Okefenokee, Land of Trembling Earth. The peat is rooted loosely. Now and then the roots snap and patches of the land break off. If you walk on one of these newborn islands, you feel the trembling that the Indians felt. And if you look around, you will see what they saw: cypresses bearded in Spanish moss. The dark mirror of water dyed eerily black by bog acid. The long shimmering of an alligator's wake. Here, in majestic slowness, flow two rivers. The Suwannee, the river that became a song, empties into the Gulf of Mexico. The St. Marys, which rises in the dark waters of the swamp, ends at the Atlantic.

61

A brown pelican perches on a Sarasota dock and royal terns return to a Cape Canaveral beach after fishing at sea.

Where marsh meets tide, the shore begins, guarded by islands of rumpled beauty. The islanders are sparse, but the families are well rooted, like the sea oats of the dunes, and wildlife is plentiful. Fiddler crabs scamper up and down the beach. Pelicans skim over the spray, and royal terns dart down to snatch a morsel from a pelican's gaping pouch or a silversides from the surface of the water. Along the outer strand of Cape Hatteras, after their fall migration, multitudes of whistling swans and snow geese grace the chill sky.

Like this wild place set apart and edged by the sea, the whole of the South is a kind of island, bounded by the Atlantic to the east, the Mississippi to the west, the Chesapeake and Susquehanna to the north, the Gulf of Mexico to the south. Seen from aloft, the South's seamless parts—the scalloped shore, the river-laced coastal plain, the rocky Piedmont, the long spine of the Appalachians, the rolling bluegrass country—emphasize the luxuriance and the rich variety of the land of the South, a region favored by nature to endure.

SOUTHERN

ALMANAC

STATES OF THE REGION

Alabama — *Yellowhammer State*
Arkansas — *Land of Opportunity*
Delaware — *First State*
Florida — *Sunshine State*
Georgia — *Peach State*
Kentucky — *Bluegrass State*
Louisiana — *Pelican State*
Maryland — *Old Line State*
Mississippi — *Magnolia State*
North Carolina — *Tarheel State*
South Carolina — *Palmetto State*
Tennessee — *Volunteer State*
Virginia — *The Old Dominion*
West Virginia — *Mountain State*

SIGN OF THE BOAR

The wild boar and its cousin the pig have long been the animals appointed by nature to appear at banquets. Served on a silver platter, pit-roasted pork is fit for a king. Tender meat and a delicate flavor probably led early restaurateurs in the South to use the pig or boar on painted tavern signs, a promise of fine fare within.

DOGGONE DAYS

We often complain about the "dog days of August," but few people know that the phrase refers to the season when Sirius, the dog star, rises with the sun. Many strange beliefs revolved around this period — that rain on the first dog day foretold forty days of rain, that dogs were more likely to go mad during these days, and that it was especially dangerous to go swimming then. Today, "dog days" usually means just that it's miserably hot!

PATCHWORK 'POSSUM

The opossum, our only pouched mammal, is such an odd-looking creature that early settlers couldn't quite figure it out. It seemed like a patchwork animal, made of leftover pieces from all the others. One man described it as having a head like a pig, a tail like a rat, the body of a fox, hands and feet like a monkey and, under its belly, a bag to carry its young.

FLORA'S PETRIFIED FOREST

A petrified forest in Flora, Mississippi? Yes! The only one east of the Mississippi River contains logs six feet across and sixty feet long. Floods from the north deposited the relics some thirty-six million years ago, but they remained buried until the mid-1800's, when erosion began to expose them.

EGGSHELLS ARE FOR THE BIRDS

At egg-laying time, mama bird is desperately in need of calcium, the stuff eggshells are made of. Some birds, particularly blue jays, resort to eating other birds' eggs to get the needed mineral. You can help provide calcium by mixing crushed chicken eggshells with

regular birdseed. Even insect-eating martins benefit from crushed eggshells sprinkled on the ground under their houses. They recognize the shells right away, and shells are the only food offering they will accept.

TALL TALES

According to down-south wisdom, killing squirrels with BB shot will ruin your squirrel stew. The only squirrel worth eating is one shot squarely in the left eye. Legend also has it that *real* pros don't shoot the squirrel at all. They aim at the branch it's standing on so that flying bark will kill the animal by concussion. Squirrel hunters have to be hardy souls, though, as everyone knows that the squirrels protect themselves by pact with mosquitos. That's the truth! The pesky little varmints agree to torment a hunter so bad he can't stand still long enough to take a shot.

A GEM OF A SALVE

Jewelweed, or silverleaf, gets its name from its water-resistant leaves that, held under water, reflect light like a mirror. Many people also know it as "touch-me-not" because its ripe seed pods explode at the slightest touch, flinging seeds far and wide. Catch them if you can! They have a pleasant nutty taste.

Jewelweed is easy to recognize in the woods. Look along moist forest borders for pretty orange or yellow snapdragonlike flowers on stalks three to four feet tall. Often, jewelweed is found near poison ivy, and—luckily for us—the thick juice of jewelweed's stems is a perfect salve for poison ivy blisters.

SWIM RABBIT SWIM

Marsh and swamp rabbits of the southern wetlands are accomplished swimmers! While cottontails usually head for water only when forced, these coastal cousins

take the plunge quite voluntarily. They sometimes escape pursuers by diving into water and swimming away or remaining submerged and motionless, with only their noses above water.

PERSIMMON PUDDING

Persimmons are extraordinarily rich in vitamin C, potassium and iron, which makes this pudding as nutritious as it is tasty. These small fruits are extremely acrid before they ripen, so wait until after the first hard frost to pick them—or you'll be puckered up for hours! The sweetness of the ripe fruits varies greatly from tree to tree, so it pays to be selective.

2 cups persimmon pulp
¾ cup honey (wild if possible)
2 cups whole wheat flour
2 cups milk
1 egg, lightly beaten
1 tsp cinnamon
½ tsp baking soda
2 tbl each hot water and butter

Mix together the first 6 ingredients, beating after each addition. Dissolve the soda in hot water and stir in. Melt the butter in a 2½ quart casserole and coat the sides. Pour in the pudding and mix with the butter. Cover and bake 1½ hours at 350°. Pudding is very moist. Serve with whipped cream or ice cream.

THE MIDWEST

by ROBERT P. CARR

What a joy it must have been for the newly arrived settlers when they stepped on the thick, sweet soil of the upper Ohio River valley. After struggling over rumpled Appalachian ridges, these westward-bound farmers must have gazed in grateful wonder across those thousand-some miles of softly rolling fertility: the Midwest. Could they possibly have imagined that this expanse of forest and prairie in but a dozen decades would become a landscape of wood-lots and wheatfields, feed a nation and then some, house great cities, and still have room for wildlife?

The Midwest is farms, the feedlot of the world. Yet amid the hustle and bustle of modern agriculture, with its towering grain silos and long rows of sun-drenched crops, wildlife has done quite well. Not through any magic of its own, mind you, but because some caring people value both land and wildlife.

A thousand miles by eight hundred miles: that's a lot of country and a lot of farms. Typically it's been the independent, family-owned farms that cover the countryside. Midwest farmers live the bucolic life—clean air and birds singing in the low morning sunshine.

I had the opportunity to learn about real work on Theron Hecht's dairy farm near Freeport, Michigan. At six every morning we were up milking the Holsteins. In winter the cows were usually a muddy mess, and their ice-caked tails were unforgettably accurate at whapping us as we leaned over to wash their udders. Some days we worked on frozen machinery, hands cracked from the cold. Then all too soon, in the early darkness, it was time again for milking. Snow-bound farms look picturesque to passers-by in a warm car. To me, they speak of hard labors and simple rewards.

Sheep huddle in a cold Michigan farmyard.
(Overleaf) Each stalk reflects the hot
June sun in this Kansas wheatfield.

Midwestern winters are notorious: four months of snarling, snow-spitting fury. But it's not the wind-lashed storms that put the bite in a midwestern winter; the energy and authority of a blizzard generate a warmth of excitement. It is the bone-splitting cold that keeps people home-bound, worshipping the fireplace or gathered in the kitchen with mugs of hot cocoa, reminiscing about the holidays. The real winter rules on those piercingly clear evenings when the snow scrunches beneath one's boots and the deer's breath hangs suspended.

A Wisconsin country home lighted up and ready for Christmas company.

71

How does wildlife survive this bitter, unyielding winter cold? The same way we do—with food and shelter. I recall finding a well-used porcupine den in a cozy hollow tree on the bank of the Brule River in Wisconsin. The den offered fine protection from the winds, and since there was only one entrance, any hungry predator would have to deal with the porky's quill-studded tail.

Porcupines have an insatiable "salt tooth" and often raise havoc by chewing on camp gear salty from human sweat. How satisfying it must be for them in the lean times of winter to gnaw upon discarded antlers—a source of salts and other minerals.

Some wildife simply sidestep the problems of winter by hibernating or migrating. Waterfowl

In a Minnesota forest, white-tailed deer browse near a camp while a porky gnaws a moose's antler to get mineral salts.

are a perfect example. They laze around the balmy, food-rich marshlands of the Gulf Coast while the northern latitudes congeal. Then with the warm spring winds, half of North America's ducks pass through midwestern airspace on the major flyways. The prairies of Minnesota and the Dakotas are the southern end of the continent's great duck-breeding grounds. Mallard, teal, bufflehead—their names resound with the fluidity of spring.

Wilderness is not particularly abundant in the Midwest; in a land so compatible with the plow,

The call of a loon is unforgettable when it breaks the quiet of remote wilderness lakes or marshes. (Overleaf) Mallards swim on a cattail marsh.

that is hardly surprising. When homesteaders cleared the prairie, vast grasslands became farms and pastures. In the process, many prairie animals, wildflowers and birds—with the exception of a few, like horned larks, which adapted well to open fields—suffered extensively.

Anyone searching for the wilder places inevitably turns north to the home of Superior, the big water. Northern Minnesota, Wisconsin and Michigan hold the deep north woods, offering precious isolation and irreplaceable beauty. The Boundary Waters, the Porcupine Mountains, Isle Royale: to many people these places are shrines. They feed the spirit as generously as the farmlands feed the body. With mountains, marshes and lakes, this western Lake Superior region quickly captures your heart.

Pristine areas such as the Sylvania tract near Watersmeet, Michigan, have the stillness, the

soaring eagles and the aromatic forests of larger wilderness areas, but are more approachable. With a quiet canoe you can slip past the shoreline to view wildlife from the water level. Otters may even pop up next to the boat in their playful manner, perhaps looking for a game of hide and seek.

As for me, well, I'm partial to Superior, its islands and shorelines. I like to sit on the high sandstone bluffs of the Pictured Rocks or the Apostle Islands watching the loons on the lake below. From these lofty perches, I can see the loons hunting as they swim beneath the surface of the translucent waters. With incredible speed and agility they rocket about on forays. Frequent rest stops are punctuated by their singular call, letting every creature know they are there.

In the case of Superior, *lake* is a somewhat misleading word—*giant water-being* might be more accurate. Serenely smooth today, with children hunting agates along the shore, Superior tomorrow might rage with wind and waves that can and, on occasion, do snap a 1,000-foot lake freighter.

Traveling west or south from the black bear and snowshoe hare north country, the Midwest unfolds in subtle grandeur which saturates like the thick moist fog of an Iowa summer. Woodlots and wet spots. The pleasure of small adventures. Indiana brooks laced with marsh marigolds. A Missouri sunrise along the

Spring in the Midwest—pasqueflowers and horned lark hatchlings in the tallgrass prairie and a snowshoe hare in brush.

Clusters of marsh marigolds come to life close by a young great horned owl roosting in a cottonwood tree.

Mississippi. Rewarding wildlife encounters are right at hand, no long expeditions required. One is never far from a river bottom owl or the thin, soaring whistle of a goldfinch in roller coaster flight. Each tiny wood holds promise of blue-eyed Marys bathed in towhee song. As Thoreau noted, "It is not what you look at, but what you see."

From a high point, a checkerboard of fields fills the vista. The gentle nature of this nearly flat landscape allowed the settlers and their descendants to build an efficient system of roads

on a grid network. This broke the land into a series of squares or sections, one mile per side, with the farmhouses almost always located on the road—the edge of the sections. The center of the section, being farthest from the farmyard, was quite naturally the last piece of land cleared or plowed. Often it was left alone.

In the forested areas, the section center was a source of wood for fuel or building materials and of wild game for the kitchen. For needed cash, trees could be sold off to the local sawmill. In the prairie areas, the section center was more vulnerable, since plowing under prairie sod was easier than clearing forest. Most prairies and much of their wildlife disappeared, bison being killed and pronghorns being chased westward.

Yet ironically, the grid system, which made it possible to cultivate most of the land, also ensured that a certain amount of habitat would flourish to shelter and nourish wildlife. Today, the remaining section centers and their borders with fields are prime places for wildlife. In spring you can see white trilliums flowering. In the heat

A herd of bison grazes on plains
flushed with golden wildflowers.

83

An eastern meadowlark whistles its
plaintive song, as if the nearby
stand of sunflowers could hear.

of summer you can hear the jubilant chickadees that brightened your birdfeeders in winter.

More and more people today see opportunities to help wildlife recover from two centuries of habitat destruction. Now new refuges and sanctuaries shelter wildlife from the Flint Hills of Kansas to the glacial plains of Ohio to the potholed prairies of North Dakota. In certain places it is once again possible to feel the earth shake as hundreds of bison bolt at the crack of lightning, or to hear wild turkey along a secluded oak-covered ridge in the shrouded early morning glow.

The enjoyment of midwestern wildlife implies the enjoyment of fields; not the symmetrical fields of corn, nor even the warm, outgoing stands of sunflowers. Though these may appeal to a sense of orderliness, they offer little of the natural diversity needed by wildlife. Far more enticing are the hay fields which have lain fallow through several seasons. In such a place, while lying on your back in the opalescent

glow of early morning, submerged in luxuriant greenery, you begin to grasp the complexity of the surrounding web of life. Part of that web is an ongoing symphony: a prattling, tumbling stream of melody. Redwings and meadowlarks on prominent perches defend invisible kingdoms with vocal intensity. Overhead, exuberant bobolinks warble a ceaseless and infinitely variable deluge of music.

Stalking along the edges of old fields may well result in unexpected encounters with foxes, woodchucks, badgers and skunks, especially

A woodchuck and a burrowing badger keep alert even while feeding or digging.

Ring-necked pheasants find cover in roadside wheatfields of Rush County, Kansas.

when the fields border on a woodlot or a scruffy fence row. Small mammals find these places fine spots to rear their families. The brushy cover provides protection from enemies and the clearings' succulent grasses, replete with insects, mice and birds' nests, cater to a broad range of appetites. At the fields' edges, hawks perch by day, owls by night.

From my childhood I still carry the memory of such an encounter. I am moving cautiously in an overgrown field. The air is still with the pressing humidity of an oncoming storm. I am hypnotized by the whispering grasses. I take a delicate step forward, and without warning a rooster pheasant detonates at my feet in a frenzied blast of feathers and cackle. Jolted out of my trance, I fall into the grasses topsy-turvy, laughing at the surprise that would come to symbolize for me life in the rural Midwest.

MIDWEST

ALMANAC

STATES OF THE REGION

Illinois—*Prairie State*
Indiana—*Hoosier State*
Iowa—*Hawkeye State*
Kansas—*Sunflower State*
Michigan—*Wolverine State*
Minnesota—*Land of
       10,000 Lakes*
Missouri—*Show-Me State*
Nebraska—*Cornhusker State*
North Dakota—*Flickertail State*
Ohio—*Buckeye State*
South Dakota—*Coyote State*
Wisconsin—*Badger State*

PLAIN PESTS

Swarms of grasshoppers sparkled in the sky like a million slivers of metal before descending to devastate crops. That's the way it was in Minnesota in 1818. In 1877, a teaming wall of insects halted trains of covered wagons moving farther west. In 1936, clouds of grasshoppers again invaded Minnesota, Nebraska and Montana. The drama of the grasshopper invasion inspired many folk artists, resulting in such pieces as grasshopper weather vanes.

COLOR IN THE WHEAT

Like liquid gold the wheat-field lies,
  A marvel of yellow and green,
That ripples and runs,
        that floats and flies,
  With the subtle shadows,
        the change, the sheen
That plays in the golden hair of a girl.
        A cloud flies there—
        A ripple of amber—a flare
Of light follows after. A swirl
In the hollows like the twinkling feet
  Of a fairy waltzer; the colors run
  To the westward sun,
Through the deeps of the ripening wheat.

I hear the reapers' far-off hum,
  So faint and far it seems the drone
Of bee or beetle, seems to come
  From far-off, fragrant, fruity zone,
    A land of plenty, where
      Toward the sun, as hasting there,
      The colors run
      Before the wind's feet
      In the wheat.

The wild hawk swoops
  To his prey in the deeps;
The sunflower droops
  To the lazy wave; the wind sleeps;
Then, moving in dazzling links and loops,
  A marvel of shadow and shine,
A glory of olive and amber and wine,
  Runs the color in the wheat.

  —*Hamlin Garland*

A FLOCK BY ANY OTHER NAME

Flock describes any group of birds nowadays, but once upon a time many had their own special name, some quite colorful: parliament of owls, charm of finches, rafter of turkeys, spring of teals, flight of swallows, fall of woodcocks and murder of crows.

BIRDSEED BREW

Sunflower seeds, from either cultivated or wild plants, can be used for more than birdseed. A little-known recipe says that one teaspoon of ground hulls steeped for three minutes in boiling water makes a fine coffee substitute.

GHOST RIDERS IN THE SKY

If you were in a dark, deserted barn surrounded by dangling cobwebs and creaking wood when a silent white form floated past, what would your first thought be? Ghosts!! Or what if you suddenly heard a scream, or a chuckle or a rattle in a field at midnight? Again, "ghosts!!" Perhaps, but more likely you are in the company of a barn owl on the hunt. These beautiful nighttime birds fly on wings made unnervingly quiet by an ever-so-finely feathered leading edge that allows the air to flow noiselessly through instead of whistling past, as it does on the hard leading edge of most birds' wings. Barn owls appear so mysteriously they probably have done more to perpetuate ghost stories than ghosts themselves!

GET 'EM WITH GARLIC

Save your songbirds from chemical pesticides with this garlic spray: soak 3 ounces of chopped garlic in 2 teaspoons of mineral oil overnight. Slowly add 1 pint of water in which ¼ ounce of soap (not detergent) has been dissolved. To use, dilute to at least 1 part to 20 parts water. That should effectively repel a variety of flying and crawling pests without hurting your wild friends. Poking a few garlic cloves into the tunnels of bothersome moles is supposed to send those pests a-running, too.

HUNTER'S RULE

One shot, one deer; two shots, one deer; three shots, no deer.

JUICY SPRUCE GUM

Indians enjoyed chewing gum long before white men ever set foot in America. The Indians broke off chunks of sticky spruce sap after it had hardened in the air and chewed it as a thirst quencher. By the late 1800's, factory-made spruce gum was popular across the nation. Modern processes and ingredients have provided gum that is sweeter and softer, but some folks claim it just isn't as good as old-fashioned spruce gum. For them, a few companies still manufacture the real thing.

WILD RICE STUFFING

Wild rice, long a staple of Indians and outdoorsmen, can be harvested in quiet waters throughout Wisconsin, Minnesota and the Great Lakes region or purchased in natural food stores. Its delightful smoky taste goes especially well with wild duck, as in this traditional recipe:

1 cup wild rice
½ pound chestnuts
1½ tbl oil
½ cup melted butter
¼ tsp salt
⅛ tsp pepper
2 tbl minced onion

Wash rice and boil 40 min. in 3 cups water; drain. Make a ½" slit in each chestnut shell, place in oiled pan and shake to coat. Roast in 450° oven for 5 min. Cool, remove shells. Cover with boiling water and simmer, covered, 10 to 20 min. Drain and mash. Toss lightly with rice and other ingredients.

MOUNTAIN STATES

by DAVID F. ROBINSON

Uh-oh. Now I'm in trouble. All I did was pull over and get out to have a closer look at the wildflowers nodding along the fencerow. And now there's a woman yelling at me from the distant ranch house.

Wait a minute. She's smiling. "Pick some!" she calls. "Western wallflower. Help yourself!" And in ten minutes I am down the long driveway and in the modest house, admiring antique bottles and arrowheads and asking rancher and wife what it's like to live year round in the high valleys of the Rockies.

Elinore Stewart, a Denver laundress homesteading in Wyoming, answered that question a century ago. "Persons afraid of coyotes and work and loneliness," she wrote, "had better let ranching alone."

Today, as in Elinore's era, there's a passel of people up here who aren't afraid of those things.

People who like the solitude of a home a dozen miles from the nearest telephone. Who cuss the aches and calluses but would go loco living in suburbia. Who revel in summer's brief splurge of wildflowers and welcome the stranger braking for a look at them.

It wasn't always that way. The first white men into these mountains came with one aim: get rich and get out. From the crystal streams and mirror ponds the trappers dragged the playful river otter—and the beaver, that tireless lumberjack and civil engineer whose public works created whole new habitats that slowed runoff and gave thirsty uplands time to drink. Fashion's thirst for furs drove the mountain men ever deeper into the wilds until the beaver were nearly wiped out.

Next came the prospector to pan and pry what nuggets he could from the surface of the

Piles of snow-covered wagon wheels and elk horns in Trail Town, Wyoming, recall bygone days. (Overleaf) From the Silverton, originally an ore freight train, passengers can view scenic canyons and wildlife along Colorado's Animas River.

94

mountains, then bore into them for more. Hard on his heels came the railroadmen, hammering down ribbons of iron through lofty pass and shadowed canyon to get supplies and miners in and the precious ores out. Trees thudded down, screeched through sawmills, and rose up again as honest buildings behind deceiving facades. Great herds of elk fell before the gun: only their antlers remained to adorn those false-fronted towns as the meat helped feed a burgeoning population. Not even the trumpeter swan evaded the sights of hunter and sportsman; early in this century, that largest of North American migratory birds had been gunned nearly to a memory.

Yet amid the exploitation, voices rose in defense of natural treasures too magnificent to plunder. In 1872, Yellowstone was set aside as the world's first national park, a chunk of Wyoming with a fringe of Montana and Idaho.

There the trumpeter builds its bulky nest at water's edge—atop a beaver lodge if one is handy—and invests its whitish eggs in a future full of hope. And there the elk multiply. Some migrate to lower pasture for the winter; others stay near the park's 10,000 thermal springs, which melt snow and ice, making it easier for the elk to push through to the food beneath.

A spurt of hot water sixty feet high and big around as his body? Haw! Nobody believed mountain man Jim Bridger's Yellowstone whopper a century ago. Yet many would believe that a bobcat's urine turned to a gemstone; why else would the secretive cat bury it to thwart the treasure seeker? And more than one observer watched river otters swim in a "train"—single file, undulating in and out of the water like dolphins—and swore up and down they'd seen a monstrous sea serpent.

A chukar partridge's striped plumage helps it hide in the grass to avoid a hungry bobcat padding about.

The folks up here love such tall tales. One old varmint sent me home half believing in an antlered rabbit called a jackalope, then sent me postcard proof of the legendary fur-bearing trout! Maybe the chukar partridge is too new an immigrant from India to have acquired a folklore here, but give 'em time. With a bird that calls its own name and runs eighteen miles an hour, they'll think of something. And their wild exaggerations will probably seem real, for in this land reality is often a wild exaggeration. Who would believe the Siamese temples, the

Their dense sleek coats enable these river
otters to take a sudden snowstorm in stride.

A close-up view of wind- and water-sculptured rocks at Bryce Canyon and Arches National Park make a hike worthwhile.

Brobdingnagian chessman, the mad sculptor's masterpieces crowding Utah's implausible erosion museum, Bryce Canyon? What youngsters could hike among the hundred weather-carved windows and bridges—one spanning nearly 300 feet—of Arches National Park and not see the handiwork of antic giants? Who could believe Wyoming's Grand Tetons, so close in the crystal air that you could put out a hand and cut your finger on their serrated edge? The beavers only doubled the impossible when they built a pond that mirrored such magnificence

and then counterpointed it with their own tiny teton of a lodge.

The Rockies that crinkle North America's western flank are youngsters, as mountains go, and the Tetons at a mere nine million years are the youngest of them. No foothills diminish the Tetons' grandeur; the Grand Teton leaps up out of Jackson Hole to claw the clouds at 13,766 feet. Settlers tried to farm the plain, but finally bowed to winter's eviction notice. Now the moose crashes through the willow brakes, the grizzly bear lords over the slopes, the cutthroat trout hooks the ardent angler, and the Steller's jay confounds birdwatchers by eluding them in its haunts among the conifers, then dropping in, bold and sassy, at *their* haunts in the picnic grounds.

What a feast for nature lovers, this range and its valley now tucked away securely as a national park. Listen: you may hear the herald horn of the trumpeter swan, a minority resident here as in Yellowstone. Now the squealing cries of an eagle, now the mutter of pronghorn hooves down in Antelope Flat, now the stereo grumble of a storm stalking the unwary vacationer from behind a blind of rock and conifer and snow.

Even some Rockies' residents fear those thunderstorms. Javelins of lightning stab out of black underbellies that seem low enough to bump your head on. Rain crashes down in curtains; crackling cannonades boom off the peaks to echo back again and again. Tree trunks shatter to toothpicks at the tickle of a lightning

A Steller's jay lands among the evergreens around a beaver pond near the Grand Tetons.

High rocky ledges give the marmot
and cougar great vantage points.

bolt. Whooshing winds finally tear the cloud.
The sun squeezes through, the rain reddens—
and you've "seen it rainin' fire in the sky."
Then the storm sputters off like an old home-
steader's woman, dragging her skirts of rain
down over the Front Range and out onto the
prairie far below. You can watch her go for fifty,
maybe one hundred miles. "A man kin see so
much farther in that country," Jim Bridger said.

And the cougar seems to know it. The big
cat hunkers down on a favorite outcrop, licks a
paw, yawns extravagantly, and watches the vast
amphitheater below for a flicker of movement.
Its tail tip beckons as if it could entice any mule
deer in its twenty-five-square-mile domain to
come closer, come closer. . . .

As settlers came closer, fearing for their
livestock, they drove the cougar from its ancient
haunts all across the land. Now it survives only
in the remotest wilds. So the marmot is in little
danger from the few cats that remain. Still, the
chunky rodent suns itself not far from a safe
crevice, for the eagle also owns a keen eye and a
sharp claw.

That sun must feel good to the marmot after
a long winter in the deathlike sleep of hiber-
nation. Mountain folk seeing him lounging
in a grassy meadow or on a rocky ledge feel a
kinship, for they have stayed awake to endure
the numbing rake of winds at 30° below, and
they too are glad to welcome the spring.

"What spring?" snorts a Colorado rancher.
"We git three months a year up here: July,
August, and winter."

Spring, for the high meadow plants, is a quick thrust skyward as soon as the snow breaks, a rush to blossom and go to seed before it's winter again. Lupine spires festoon the carpet at the feet of mountains the Indians called "hoary-headed fathers." Mule deer munch through fields sequined with blossoms as if in celebration. And far below in sagebrush country the sage grouse plucks the evergreen leaves for food or feasts on grasshoppers and ants. Lewis and Clark dubbed this bird the "Cock of the Plains." It's as western as the American cowboy.

Summer visitors to Wyoming may happen upon lupines in bloom, mule deer amid wildflowers or a sage grouse in scrub.

Cowboys driving cattle by the hundreds
still cut trails through the sagebrush.

Tall in the saddle. Quick on the draw. How
those images have dramatized the cowboy's long
reign as our nation's favorite folk hero! The
heroics are faded tintypes now, compared with
those of days when pioneers staked out ranches
and turned the herds out to graze.

Summer's end was, and still is, roundup time.
Get 'em moving, down the trail from pasture in
Montana to Wyoming for branding and shipping
to market in the fall. Point riders lead the way.
Flank riders hold the sides. Drag riders and
cowdogs bring up the rear, keep the laggards
moving, eat the herd's dust. Pronghorn, elk,
mule deer look up to watch 'em plod by. Maybe
the mule deer will spook, bolting away upslope
in the typical jumps or "stots" that take all four
feet off the ground. Or maybe the herd will
spook, giving the cowpokes a stampede to
quell—and a bellowing stray calf to be wrestled
onto a rider's saddle and returned to the herd.

Three days to go maybe fifty miles. Seems
like five hundred. Rattlers. Scorpions. Dust.
Smell. Bones and spirits get saddle-weary. But,
ah-h-h, then the night sends its cool and starry
benediction. If the herd is quiet, you might have
time to gaze up and watch for a shooting star

sizzling toward the horizon or the rarely visible aurora borealis throwing lasers at the heavens.

Once prairie dogs by the millions ate the grass and pocked the plains with burrows in their seemingly endless communities called "towns." Their constant burrowing did keep the soil healthy and aerated, but they also ate the cattle's food. And a horse or cow could step into a burrow and snap a leg bone. So the towns were flooded and the prairie dogs poisoned, 'till only scattered colonies remained.

One prairie dog town seems to be posting a constant guard by Devils Tower in northeastern Wyoming. The lava plug of an ancient volcano long since stripped of the softer soil that covered it, the tower thrusts up some 865 feet and fairly begs for legends. Thus: seven Indian girls, chased by bears, jumped on a low rock—which saved them by rising into a pillar while the frustrated bears clawed those deep grooves in its flanks. Geology and mythology. Amid the wonders of the mountain states, both seem right at home.

What can imagination make of the marvels of Yellowstone? Jim Bridger kept his in check as he told of pools aboil—but he was hooted at anyway. Let yours run free; can it see only algae tinting the throat of a geothermal vent? Or does it see a hint of the color and shape of a morning glory blossom in Morning Glory Pool?

Without knowing it, Bridger had been one of the first explorers to see the greatest area of thermal activity on the planet. Now millions come to see and photograph the gallery of geysers and pools and the wildlife. If their timing is right, they may glimpse the elk, the lordly deer that once shared the continent with Indian hunters; Shawnees called them *wapiti*. In the fall

Geology went wild in the West, forming Devils Tower, home of this prairie dog, and Yellowstone's Morning Glory Pool.

you can hear the big bulls bugling, challenging all comers for possession of a harem. By displays, threats, and sometimes by clash of antlers, dominance among the males is decided—and maintained even after the rut as bulls adjourn to bachelor clubs.

Lucky is the rancher who can look out a window and see elk grazing on his spread; luckier still is the hunter who can bag one during the limited season. Yet the fact that there's a season at all is proof of the elk's comeback, though never again will the elk reach the numbers it once could muster.

Never again: how that phrase haunts the mountain states. "Idaho is what America was," a T-shirt proclaims. Yet parts of Idaho and its neighbors have repeatedly been the floor of seas and once of immense Lake Bonneville. You can pick up fossil seashells in the deserts of Nevada, see ancient shorelines terracing the slopes near Salt Lake City, watch speed machines streak across the pavement of salt left behind as Lake Bonneville went up in vapor. Never again a seafloor? Wait a few million years.

Never again will gold-hungry, silver-seeking miners burrow like prairie dogs, calling their digs

A bull elk bugles a warning to any bull within earshot as he escorts his harem up the forested slope.

Whether it's a three-day pack trip or a summer-long stay in a cabin, the Rockies promise bold scenery, bracing air and a chance to see mountain wildlife. (Overleaf) The ever-alert pronghorn will dart away wildly at the slightest alarm.

the Little Dora, the Old Lout, the Terrible, or their towns Eureka, Fairplay, Goldfield. Never again will gunslingers duel like wapiti, nor Indians gallop the grasslands like pronghorns. Yet remnants of all these remain. Miners still dig, actors still sling blanks on movie sets and in tourist cowtowns, pronghorns still nibble beneath purple mountain majesties, ever ready to spring away. And into this wrinkled rock garden, this swatch of grass and stand of aspen and sprinkle of sand and snow, humankind will ever come, seeking silence, solace, self.

MOUNTAIN

ALMANAC

STATES OF THE REGION

Colorado — *Centennial State*
Idaho — *Gem State*
Montana — *Treasure State*
Nevada — *Sagebrush State*
Utah — *Beehive State*
Wyoming — *Equality State*

CAT-OF-THE-MOUNTAINS

In the days of pioneers, the mountain lion stalked its prey all across the country, from Eastern woodlands, across prairies, to Pacific shores. *Painter, panther, puma, cougar, el leone* and *catamount* — all are names for this big wildcat. Another name, *varmint,* recalls early Americans' feelings for the animal. It was feared and cursed.

Bounty hunters took a heavy toll on the mountain lion population. So did loss of habitat. This once free-roaming cat is now limited to eleven Western states and Texas with a remnant population in the Florida Everglades and Big Cypress Swamp.

BITE THE DUST

Whenever anyone complains about dusty cars or furniture, remind them of May 9, 1934, when strong winds swirled soil from the plains in Montana and Wyoming into the air. High-altitude winds carried about 350 million tons of this earth eastward. By evening, 12 million tons had fallen like snow on Chicago. By May 11, the 100-mph winds had taken the dust to Boston, New York and Washington. But it didn't stop there! For several days afterward, sailors on ships in the Atlantic, some 300 miles off the coast, complained about dusty decks.

WOLFING IT DOWN

Beautiful lupines acquired a ferocious name, from the Latin *lupus*-wolf, because people thought that the flowers stole nutrients from the soil the way wolves steal sheep. Actually, lupines improve the soil in which they grow by fixing free nitrogen.

BY THE DARK OF THE MOON

Check the phases of the moon before your next wildlife-watching trip, if you believe the words of some old-time mountain men. They say the best time to see deer, coyote, foxes and the like is during the dark of the moon: the week before and after the new moon. Why? Supposedly, animals will feed and travel at night if the moon is full; but when the dark nights of the new moon come, animals rest at night and are out and about more often when wildlife watchers can see them — during the early morning and evening hours.

IT'S AGAINST THE LAW

It's against the law of physics to sink in the Great Salt Lake in Utah. Since the Pleistocene glaciers retreated, 95 percent of the large freshwater lake that covered parts of Utah, Nevada and Idaho has evaporated. The evaporation caused the water's salt content to increase to 28 percent, making it eight times saltier than ocean water. Swimmers are so buoyant they simply cannot sink.

TEENY TINY DINOSAURS

Diplodocus dinosaurs, seventy-five-and-a-half-feet long, were dug up in northeastern Utah in the early 1900's in a find called the greatest concentration of dinosaurs in the world. But some of the reptiles found in the dig were pipsqueaks in comparison. The *Laosaurus* was only two-and-a-half-feet long, and the *Hoplosuchus* didn't reach the eight-inch mark on a ruler!

OUT WHERE THE WEST BEGINS

Out where the hand-clasp's
a little stronger,
Out where the smile dwells
a little longer,
That's where the West begins;
Out where the sun is a little brighter,
Where the snows that fall
are a trifle whiter,
Where the bonds of home
are a wee bit tighter,
That's where the West begins.

Out where the skies are a trifle bluer,
Out where the friendship's a little truer,
That's where the West begins;
Out where a fresher breeze is blowing,
Where there's laughter
in every streamlet flowing,
Where there's more of reaping
and less of sowing,
That's where the West begins.

Out where the world is in the making,
Where fewer hearts in despair are aching,
That's where the West begins;
Where there's more of singing
and less of sighing,
Where there's more of giving
and less of buying,
And a man makes friends
without half trying,
That's where the West begins.

—Arthur Chapman

PIÑON NUT SOUP

Piñon or pine nuts are relished by wildlife and people alike. The sweet tasting seeds from the Rocky Mountain nut pine and the one-leaved nut pine have been used in place of wheat by some Indian tribes, who also collect them for commercial sale. The nuts are gathered in two ways: by sweeping the area under the pines and separating the seed from the debris, and by raiding the nests of pack rats, who store pine nuts for winter. The nuts can be eaten raw or roasted and can be substituted in almost any recipe calling for nuts. Here's a recipe for piñon soup that can be eaten chilled or steaming hot:

Simmer 2 cups milk, 1 cup chicken stock, 1 cup raw piñon nuts, 1 small diced onion, a few sprigs of mint and 1/8 tsp freshly ground pepper for half an hour, stirring occasionally. Process in a blender until smooth, then reheat for immediate use or refrigerate and serve cold. Garnish with minced chives to enhance the flavor.

THE SOUTHWEST

by WAYNE BARRETT

The sun-scorched colors of a summer sky lingering long past supper . . . the front porch swing creaking its constant complaint . . . lightning bugs glowing in a Mason jar. Memories from back home in Oklahoma.

Memories, too, of the biting cold of a blue norther. "Nothing between here and the North Pole but a 'bob-war' fence," my grandma used to say. "And it's down."

Another time of year, I remember the tornado howling its warning, driving us to a tomblike cellar, then screeching and tearing through the elms and sucking paving bricks from Main Street. I vowed never to smoke again, or say bad words. And I didn't, for a while.

Tales—sometimes on the tall side—of dust storms, blazing heat and drought give outsiders an incomplete picture of life in desert country.

It's true that rain seldom comes to the desert. In west Texas a five-inch rainfall is five drops an inch apart, one joke says. But when rain does come, it's likely to pour down in a cloudburst, and poppies may suddenly bloom to spread carpets of gold. And the air is so clear that you can see the blooms across those wide-open spaces for miles.

From the wind-swept plains of Oklahoma and Texas to the deserts of Arizona and New Mexico, man, animals and plants wage what John Steinbeck calls the "war of sun and dryness against living things." In this war, "the gray and dusty sage wears oily armor to protect its inward small moistness. Some plants engorge themselves with water in the rare rainfall and store it. . . . Animal life wears a hard, dry skin or an outer skeleton to defy the dessication."

Thick-walled adobes in Taos make ideal homes—
built from the land they stand on—in this
perpetually sunny climate.
(Overleaf) A bumper crop of California poppies
colors the desert after a rare rain.

124

Humans, too, have devised ways to outwit the heat. In the 16th century, Indians built thick-walled houses of adobe and worked in comfort grinding corn, weaving baskets and making pottery. Today air-conditioning cools even the thinnest glass-walled homes.

Some modern Indians, the Zunis, Hopis, Navajos, Papagos and Pimas, trying to preserve their cultures' frail bonds, continue to live on the harsh desert. They live "off" the desert as well, hunting game and reaping the juicy, sweet fruit of saguaro cactus. The saguaro matures slowly

Magenta, juicy and sweet, the fruit of the saguaro cactus attracts a Papago Indian and a desert cactus wren.

In the desert, a mourning dove nests
safely in its nest on a cholla cactus,
and a rattler counters a coyote's threats.

and at 150 years may tower 50 feet and weigh 8 tons, most of it stored water. In its candelabralike branches cactus wrens forage, hawks and owls roost, Gila woodpeckers and flickers chisel nest holes.

Widespread in both the Sonoran desert in southern Arizona and the Chihuahuan desert that straddles the Rio Grande grows a less hospitable cactus—cholla. Small, thorny branches of the cactus, so legend says, actually leap at passers-by. A warning to people tempted to savor *its* pear-shaped fruit! Despite the cholla's

A Gila monster defeats "dragon slayers" with a poisonous bite; the horned toad feigns fierceness with daggerlike scales.

reputation, wrens and mourning doves nest secure and comfortable among its spines. Elsewhere in the Southwest's desert lands other rugged plants add their special color—ocotillos wave long, willowy wands tipped with crimson flowers; ground-hugging yuccas and sotols sprout bayonetlike leaves.

Harsh desert habitat does not seem to bother the ubiquitous coyote, even when sharing the right of way with a prairie rattlesnake. Or the smaller sidewinder. Moving sideways, as its name suggests, the sidewinder escapes midday heat by seeking shade under a cactus, burying all but its head in the sand.

The Gila monster is built for the starkness of desert life. It does well on a diet of hatchlings, young rabbits and eggs. If necessary, the slow-moving lizard, living off its fat, can go many months between meals.

Deep in the Grand Canyon, water is a drawing card for migratory snowy egrets and resident bighorn sheep.

The roadrunner, local fast-stepping bird that is often a symbol of the Southwest, races for its desert meals. This ever-hungry cousin of the cuckoo outruns insects, mice, lizards, horned toads and snakes. The bird may tenderize a reptile by seizing it with its bill and repeatedly slamming it against a rock.

A part-time visitor to the region—the snowy egret—makes a fueling stopover in the Grand Canyon on its migration route. Human visitors to the Southwest stop in this mighty gorge not to eat, drink and rest, but to gape. The Grand Canyon dazzles the eye with chameleon colors and boggles the mind with immense dimensions.

Carved by time and the Colorado River, the Grand Canyon plunges almost 6,000 feet at its deepest, gapes 18 miles at its widest, and stretches in length more than 200 miles. The first time I stood at the edge and looked down

132

that awesome chasm, as many visitors must, I had the urge to race back to the nearest tree and hug it for dear life!

Along the Canyon's rim, tassel-eared squirrels climb ponderosa pines to chatter to their neighbors, desert sparrows and horned toads sun on rocks, desert bighorn sheep scramble down cliffs to browse on scrub and grasses. During rutting season, from summer into fall, visitors may witness rival rams charging head-on at incredible speeds dozens of times. Bathers escape the heat of the canyon in a refreshingly

cool, terraced natural pool in the swirling waters of Havasu Creek, a tributary of the Colorado.

Not far from the Canyon in the northeast corner of Arizona, the cliff dwellings of Montezuma Castle National Monument recall a more primitive way of life in a distant age. An entire farming community, part of a culture called *Sinagua,* which means "without water," died out in the 1400's, possibly because it was unable to meet the challenge of the sun.

In modern times, man's ingenuity has changed that old way of life dictated by geology and climate. Now in numerous parts of the Southwest, artificial lakes, created by damming the many rivers that flow through the region, give relief from withering weather. Sailing, waterskiing and fishing are popular sports in areas that formerly were isolated and parched. To nourish lawns, fill swimming pools and water vegetable gardens, man has built irrigation canals and tapped underground water sources. These aquifers, or natural reservoirs, have been fed drop by precious drop from rainfall for hundreds of centuries. As yet, we don't know for certain the consequences of using that water to create a lush countryside out of the arid sunbelt.

Bathers play in the falls of Havasu Canyon, home of the Havasupai—"people of the blue-green water"—a stark contrast to centuries of silence at Montezuma Castle.

(Overleaf) Greater sandhill cranes take
wing after a cornfest near the Rio Grande.

Great flocks of sandhill cranes are attracted to
the shallow lakes of treeless flatlands in
New Mexico and west Texas, which Spaniards
dubbed *Llano Estacado*— Staked Plain.
Before homesteaders came to stake claims and
build fences, bison roamed this land, fattening on
its short grass. Now bison have retreated to
refuges, but jackrabbits and prairie dogs remain;
and farther east, in Big Thicket country, the
armadillo thrives.

The Texas coast, fringed with barrier islands,
shows the face of more gentle Southwest sands.

On Padre Island National Seashore, yellow
primroses gild dunes, and ghost crabs skitter
across the sand to forage on incoming tides.
Raucous laughing gulls call out hoarse *hah-hah-
hahs* to claim fishing rights as they dunk their
heads in the food-filled shallows.

Throughout the Southwest from Arizona to
Oklahoma—a beguiling tapestry of desert and
seashore, mountains and canyons and open
plains—wildlife and man skirmish in the constant
war of sun and dryness against living things.
Wildlife survives with instinct and amazingly

A hiker or hunter may interrupt an armadillo rooting for grubs, or flush the wary
jackrabbit hiding in wildflowers.

The roots of primroses help to hold back the dunes on Padre Island, Texas, where laughing gulls squabble and ghost crabs scurry across the sand.

adapted bodies. Man copes with humor and perseverance. With time, man even comes to love that country that at first seems harsh. For once you get used to it, the desert takes on a special beauty, the home folks say. Ask anyone who lives there if he'd trade those cloudless black starry skies, those fiery sunsets, that hazeless air, those flamboyant flowering cacti, those coyotes that howl in the night. And would he leave those free wide-open spaces? Never! Southwestern folk mean to stay put . . . the good Lord willin' and the creeks don't rise.

SOUTHWEST

ALMANAC

STATES OF THE REGION

Arizona—*Grand Canyon State*
New Mexico—*Sunshine State*
Oklahoma—*Sooner State*
Texas—*Lone Star State*

LIZARDS A-PLENTY

Native Indian craftsmen feature many Southwest lizards in drawings and on pottery and woven baskets. Understandably so, because lizards are fascinating creatures.

Imagine—the chuckwalla escaping enemies by puffing up to lodge itself in a rock crevice, the horned toad frightening foes by squirting blood from its eyes, the venomous Gila monster baring its vicious teeth, the racerunner lizard taking off at a gallop, the Mearn's rock lizard scaling almost vertical walls of rock and the acrobatic large-crested lizard raising its upper body and jogging off lickety-split across the desert on its hind legs.

HAPPY NAVAITA!

For the Papago Indians, the first day of the New Year is early in the summer—the time of the saguaro harvest, or *Navaita*. Some of the *pitahaya,* or saguaro fruit, is eaten raw, some is boiled down to a thick, amber-colored syrup and some is dried in the sun for winter use. The Southwest Indians welcome their New Year with— what else?—a fermented saguaro wine.

U.S. CAMEL CORPS

In 1856, the U.S. Army imported 75 camels to Texas for use on desert reconnaissance missions. The camel was the perfect beast for the job: it did not need to carry food or water and was stronger and faster than a horse or mule. The Army declared the experiment a success, but plans to reinforce the Corps with 1,000 animals were set aside during the Civil War.

Some of the camels already here were sold to miners, others were left to roam. Cowboys and mule skinners detested the camels' haughty appearance, loud moaning and awkward gait and the inevitable stampede whenever a horse or mule got a whiff of them. Eventually all the camels were shot or died off, ending a camel era that never really got started.

OPHIDIOPHOBIA

The Southwest is home for 17 of the 30 species of rattlesnake found in the United States, plus the venomous Arizona coral snake. That makes most of us who have a touch of ophidiophobia—fear of snakes—pretty uncomfortable. We shouldn't be. Poisonous snakes cause fewer than ten deaths per year in the United States.

ROADRUNNER

Out of the western chaparral
  Where the raw, new highways run,
He flashes swift as a rainbow flame
  And races the morning sun.
He perks and preens with lifted crest,
  He dances, heel and toe.
He will jig and flirt in the
    roadway dirt—
Then—off like a shot he'll go.

—Sharlot M. Hall

FOUR-BY-FOUR

Armadillos, those outlandish, lumbering tanks of the mammal world, reproduce in a way as strange as their looks. For the nine-banded armadillo, the only species that lives in the United States, mating occurs late in the summer. The fertilized egg lies dormant until about November, and the young are born in spring. This species always bears identical quadruplets—the only mammal known to do so consistently.

TORNADO ALLEY

Texas and Oklahoma form the southern end of "Tornado Alley." Scientists believe that tornadoes are common in the central United States because topography sets the stage for the collision of two major air masses: the first one travels down off the Rocky Mountains and is cool and dry; the second one moves north from the Gulf of Mexico and is warm and very humid. Normally, when cool and warm air meet, the heavy cool air simply slides under the warm air. But since the cool air is coming off the mountains, it falls over the warm air and traps it. Somehow, the two layers must exchange positions. A bubble of warm air may form and rise through the cool layer, pulling a column of air behind it. The earth's spin adds a twist and a tornado is born.

ROASTING-EAR BREAD

For a corn bread with special texture and flavor, add some freshly grated corn to your favorite recipe. Use one ear for a 9" by 5" pan of bread.

NATURAL NECTAR

Rosy-red, naturally tart sumac* punch is a variation of the pioneers' "Indian lemonade." Serve over ice with a slice of lemon and a sprig of spearmint.

2 quarts of water
1 cup ripe sumac berries
1 tbl whole cloves
4 one-inch sticks cinnamon, broken up
1½ to 2 cups sugar

1. Bring water to a boil; add berries, cloves and cinnamon; return to a boil. Cover, lower heat and simmer for 15 minutes.
2. Strain through a sieve lined with damp cheesecloth.
3. Add sugar to taste and chill. Serve cold. Makes about 2 quarts.

*The fuzzy conical clusters of the edible staghorn sumac cannot possibly be confused with the drooping white berries of poison sumac.

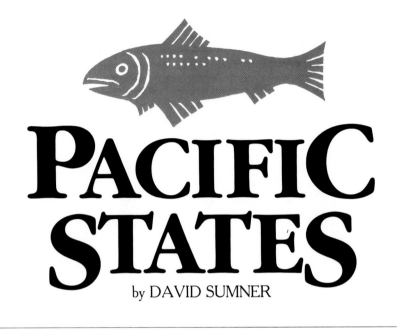

PACIFIC STATES

by DAVID SUMNER

Foaming blue surf pounding rock, frothy wavelets lapping a beach, fog like a veil drifting from sea over land. This is the edge of our continent, the Pacific states.

For the most part, this edge is decisive. From Washington's Cape Flannery, south along Oregon's rock-studded shore, to below California's Big Sur, jutting headlands and sheer cliffs front the sea. "One long battle line," this has been called, where waves that first swell 6,000 miles away crash in a final, battering assault against the land.

Listen to the sounds, watch the motion of the waves and of the birds, glimpse a whale breaking the surface of a bay or harbor, and you will sense the natural poetry of the Pacific states. But take an imaginary flight for a satellite's eye view of this region and another picture emerges.

No part of the United States is more diverse than this place we call the "West Coast." If you orbited at 60,000 feet, you would see a complex mosaic: ranges of high peaks, lush inland valleys rich with crops, vast forests, ribbonlike rivers, large cities and, along the east, a zone of great deserts.

Roam this same region by car and afoot and the diversity grows. In California you can visit a site that once went without rain for 767 straight days. In Washington you can stand in a cool forest soaked by over 140 inches of rain a year. Crossing the California Sonoran desert, you will see plants and animals common in Mexico. Hiking a 14,000-foot peak, you'll find life forms like those on Alaska's North Slope.

Everywhere in the Pacific states, you will find refreshing variety—and also sudden marvelous contrasts. Where might you see a whale offshore and a bear in a single glance? Perhaps on a

The fin of this killer whale slices through the
water at the busy, very civilized Seattle harbor.
(Overleaf) Oregon at the sea—the Coast Range
spills into the Pacific in a tumble of rocks.

146

Strollers on a California beach may spy
a sea otter offshore resting in a kelp
bed or a starfish clinging to a rock.

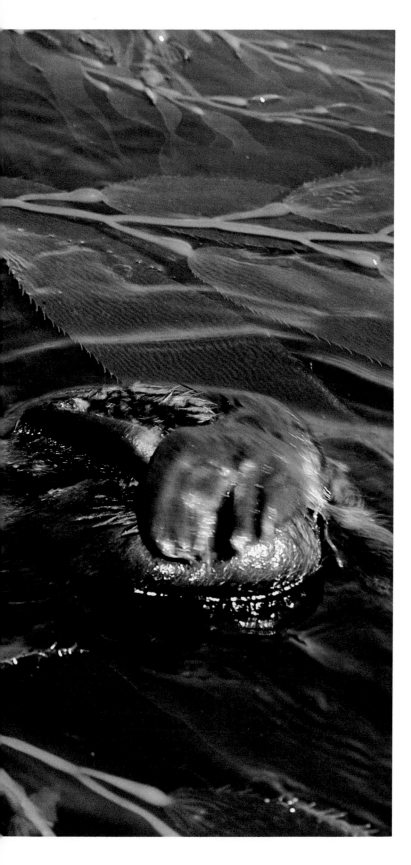

stroll along a Washington beach where a black
bear has shambled down to the sea to feed on
the remains of a sea lion washed ashore after a
killer whale attack.

And where might you find a sea otter and a
starfish close by? Perhaps just off a Pacific point
where the otter's cat-whiskered face bobs in the
waves, not far from rocks where a bright starfish
stands out in a child's fantasy world of color.
Less than a foot from the starfish is a brilliant
green anemone, waving like an underwater
flower. Sea urchins and sea slugs, hermit crabs

149

and sponges, chitons and snails: all jostle together in the waves.

Here on the rocks between the tides, it almost seems as if too much life is crowded into too little space. But remember it all fits together. The sea otter would like nothing better than to have the sea urchin for supper, and the hermit crab is looking for an empty snail shell to make its home. Farther down the shoreline, a small group of harbor seals, dark eyes bulging, take a belly-whopper into the sea on a foray for prime fare: fish, octopus, squid and other small marine

Harbor seals take the plunge to feed near Point Reyes lighthouse, California.

animals. But the shore is much more than a place for looking. Picnickers frequent Oregon's seventy-five seaside state parks; beachcombers wade in the numbing waters of California's Point Reyes National Seashore or dig for clams on beaches up and down the coast. Clam diggers methodically work their way along the ocean's edge, plunging their long forks into the sand every two inches or so until they uncover enough clams to fill their buckets.

Many Pacific beaches are close to towns or even large cities. San Franciscans are especially lucky, for but a short walk from the city bus lines are the restful sandy shores of the Golden Gate National Recreation Area.

For those with a yen for the sea, the breeze is often just right for an afternoon's sail in the protected waters of San Francisco Bay. Adventuresome birdwatchers occasionally boat out to the offshore Farallon Islands, one of America's very first national wildlife refuges. "The fascinating Farallones," they have been called, and the phrase is apt, particularly in spring and fall. This is the largest Pacific seabird

Lucky youngsters strike a clam bed on an
Oregon sand bar and San Franciscans take
a holiday sail near Golden Gate Bridge.

rookery south of Alaska. Here tens of thousands of cormorants, oystercatchers, puffins and gulls shadow the landscape. Overhead, the quick, rhythmic "foof-foof" sounds of these birds' wingbeats break the silence. Follow a puffin ashore with your binoculars, and you'll see it vanish into a rocky niche to deliver food to its young. Scan the horizon, too, for you may catch sight of a pod of spouting gray whales on their regular migrations between Alaska and Baja.

The Pacific Coast is wet, but inland—across the green coastal mountains, across the rich farm valleys, and over the high passes through the Sierras and Cascades—life spreads thin or clusters around oases like Mono Lake east of Yosemite. At Mono Lake, during spring and fall migrations, a dizzying swirl of over 800,000 birds may gather in a single day. Most are gulls and stilt-legged shorebirds (phalaropes, sand-pipers, killdeer), but over one hundred species have been noted. If the swirl is mostly killdeer, the dizzying sight can also become deafening with a shrill chorus of *kill-dee, kill-dee, kill-dee* that seems to echo the bird's name.

Flocking killdeer find Mono Lake's sandy flats a rich late-summer feeding spot.

154

Farther south, China Lake is no lake at all; it is all but bone dry. Increasing water consumption in the Los Angeles area probably caused the water table to fall, leaving only scattered seeps and springs. But this is all the desert life here needs. Cacti and geckos, whiptail lizards and horned toads: each has its place. So do some 40 fleet wild horses that must compete with over 4,000 wild burros for China Lake's meager but nourishing plant life.

In sharp contrast with the deserts, California's interior valleys, nearer the sea, are among the world's richest croplands. The Imperial and Central Valleys grow everything from cotton to lettuce to melons. Napa Valley is famous for its fine wines.

So the Pacific states' diversity continues, with each area, like patches of a quilt, colorful in its own special way. Back along California's

Tourists and natives alike find the tranquil Spanish missions, with their rolling vineyards, doves and peaceful churches, a welcome respite from city life.

(Overleaf) A wild horse gallops across the dried bed of China Lake.

golden coast, the moderating presence of the sea cools the southern shore, warms the north, and brings vital rain to both.

South down the coast from San Francisco lies a narrow band of land that to the Spanish of the late 1700's seemed like paradise on earth. Here the early padres built a string of twenty-one missions, conveniently spaced one day's journey, by donkey, apart. Santa Cruz, San Luis Obispo, Santa Barbara, San Diego: all began as small mission settlements.

Today these historic landmarks remain as retreats for people as well as havens for birds unable to adapt to sunny California's more crowded towns and sprawling cities. Of these missions, none is more famous than San Juan Capistrano, south of Los Angeles, where the cliff swallows return regularly from South America, usually on March 19. Here too you will find gentle white doves, symbols of peace and love, adding to the hallowed mood of the historic mission.

North of the Bay area stretches a contrasting world, cooler and wetter than the strip to the

south. Here, from one to thirty miles inland, the Pacific states' most famous tree, the giant coast redwood, makes its last stand. Especially in Redwood National Park, near Crescent City, these 200-foot tall (and taller) monarchs form hushed cathedral groves just as serene as the old missions to the south. Even woodland sounds — the chatter of a chickaree squirrel, the tattoo of a woodpecker, the squawk of a jay — are quickly absorbed by the redwoods' fog-bound silence.

The redwoods are unique to one area of favorable climate and soil; they occur nowhere

Explorers walking through this California redwood forest may hear the chirping of an invisible chickaree high in a tree.

A tule elk laps water at the edge of a pond where a western grebe may be partially concealed among the rushes.

else. This special adaptation to a particular habitat occurs throughout the Pacific states; several distinct areas have special forms of life. The dwarf tule elk has a lighter coat than its cousins in the Rockies and Northwest. Like the redwoods, the tule elk occur nowhere else. Today this rare animal survives only in a few herds in the central valleys.

More widespread species of wildlife add their own distinctive beauty to wherever they live. Come upon a large, lowland lake with bullrushes lining its shore. Look carefully, and you may make out a beady red eye just above a spearlike bill. Their owner is most likely a western grebe, an adaptable water bird at ease rearing its young from Mexico to Canada.

Some areas of the Pacific states don't have unique species, but even so they stand out. Coastal Washington's Olympic rain forest

163

A male ruffed grouse drums for a mate
from its mossy perch in the lush Hoh
rain forest of Washington.

overflows with wonders in size and color. The
trees here are common throughout the Northwest, but ideal climate makes this a realm of
giants. In three side-by-side river valleys grow
record-sized western hemlock, Douglas fir and
red alder.

Hike on an Olympic trail in mid-summer and
you will feel almost as if you are in a sanctuary
with walls a mass of spreading ferns and
soft-hued wildflowers. Perhaps you'll spook a
chicken-sized ruffed grouse; it will take off with
a startling, feathery "boom." It will also
give you a glimpse of another Olympic phenome-
non. In these shadowy forests, many species—
the grouse, black bear, mountain lion and flying
squirrel—are darker than elsewhere. This
seems to give them better protection from their
enemies or allow them to stalk with less
chance of being seen.

As you gain elevation walking up that mountain trail, you'll notice that the trees first grow smaller, then become stunted. This is true in all the mountainous national parks of the Pacific states—North Cascades, Olympic, Mt. Rainier, Crater Lake, Kings Canyon, Yosemite— for altitude creates a climate, and a community, of its own. The trees are dwarfed compared to the groves below because high winds and biting cold thwart their growth. For similar reasons, the mountain wildflowers are brighter than those lower down. Few insects venture up to high

Family backpackers below Mt. Rainier follow a path by Indian paintbrush and, higher up, patches of snow.

On an arid flat of snow-dusted sagebrush,
a courting sage grouse puffs and utters
its deep bubbling notes.

altitudes, so the short-lived blooms must be
vivid to attract these vital pollinators.

Travel across the great mountains of
California and you reach desert; do likewise in
the Pacific Northwest and you find the same.
Yes, Washington and Oregon, usually thought
of as drenched with rain, have extensive high
desert as well. The Hart Mountain Refuge in
southern Oregon is an example. Here it seems
as if you've been transported deep into Nevada.
On these wide-open plains, swift pronghorn flow
over sagebrush, a coyote stalks a plump sage
grouse which takes flight like an overloaded
bomber, a kangaroo rat scurries for cover. And
having a chance to see all that is part of the
pleasure of exploring up and down the coast.

Roaming the teeming Pacific states provides
a kaleidoscope of all the natural wonders of this
nation. Moving ever west, pioneers found rich
forests and great valleys, high peaks and bright
deserts. Nearing the West Coast, they found
all this repeated, but intensified and enriched.
And then at last they reached the Pacific,
the counterpart of the rocky and sandy shores
from which their great westward journey began.

PACIFIC
ALMANAC

STATES OF THE REGION

California—*Golden State*
Oregon—*Beaver State*
Washington—*Chinook State*

BOUNTIFUL SALMON

The Pacific salmon, perhaps more than any other wild creature, represented the bounty of nature to West Coast Indians. Tribes welcomed the first salmon of the year with great ceremony and celebration, thanking the salmon spirits for guiding the fish up the streams. During the fishing season, members of the tribe ritually buried the salmon hearts and threw the bones back into the water because they thought that would ensure next year's return of the salmon.

The involvement with salmon did not stop with the fishing season, though. The art of the coastal Indians is rich in salmon images. The Makah, Quileute and Chinook Indians carved the fish on wooden boxes and using berry dye painted it on woven baskets and hats.

WEATHER RECORDS

California holds U.S. weather records for both the longest dry period (767 days in the Mohave Desert) and the highest recorded temperature (134°F in Death Valley). The state also holds the record for the most snowfall in a single storm: 189 inches at Mount Shasta Ski Bowl.

FISH IN THE DESERT

Nine species of fish live in the few springs and streams of awesome Death Valley desert in California. The fish aren't large, and they aren't colorful, but they manage to survive in this incredibly harsh environment. Pools of water may be small, highly saline and vary in temperature from near freezing to almost 100° F. Yet these little fish have lived in them for at least 2,000 years.

WINTER IN THE SIERRAS

The pines are black on Sierra's slope,
And white are the drifting snows,
The flowers are gone,
         the buckthorn bare,
And chilly the north wind blows;
The pine boughs creak,
And the pine trees speak
The language the north wind knows.

There's never a track leads in or out
Of the cave of the big brown bear,
The squirrels have hid
         in their deepest holes
And fastened the doors with care;
The red fox prowls,
And the lean wolf howls
As he hunts far down from the lair.

The eagle hangs on the wing all day
For the chance of a single kill,
And the little gray hawk
         hunts far and wide
Before he can get his fill.
The snow wreaths sift,
And the blown snows drift
To the canyons deep and still.
                    —*Mary Austin*

MOUNTAIN BEAVER

Wildlife watchers in the Pacific Northwest might view a curious creature found nowhere else: the mountain beaver. Despite its name, the creature isn't a beaver and doesn't live only in mountains. A burrowing rodent, it has shiny brown fur like the beaver, but no tail. It also has beaverlike teeth; but instead of gnawing bark, it nibbles tender plants such as ferns.

SANTA BARBARA AND THE SIRENS

Strange wails and cries coming from Santa Barbara Island used to terrorize crewmen heading through these California coastal waters. Convinced that mythical sirens were trying to lure them overboard to their deaths, the sailors gave the area a wide berth. Turns out, the caterwauling was just that: a horde of vociferous squabbling cats—offspring of the survivors of an ancient shipwreck.

SEAWEED SOUP

You may turn up your nose at eating seaweed, but you've probably eaten it without even knowing! Ground-up seaweed is used to improve the texture of ice cream, chocolate milk, salad dressing and pudding. Some people use seaweed in cooking. Added to a seafood stew or soup, seaweed gives a salty sea flavor.

On your next vacation at the beach, you might want to try collecting some. Dulse and laver are two of the most popular and easily identified seaweeds. Dulse varies from red to purple and has thin, deeply lobed fronds. Laver's single flat blade has ruffled edges, usually a vivid red. Both species are common in shallow coastal waters.

BLUEBERRY SOURDOUGHS

There's nothing like the smell of sourdough pancakes, or "flippers," sizzling over a fire, but who says they're only for campers? They're just as good on a leisurely Sunday morning at home! For the starter, get a large crock (never use metal) and make a smooth paste from: 2 cups flour, 1 tsp salt, 3 tbl sugar, ½ tsp dry yeast and 2 cups lukewarm water. Cover loosely and set in a warm place. Stir occasionally for two to three days, when the mixture will be bubbly and pleasantly yeast-scented. The night before you cook the hotcakes, add 2 cups flour and 2 cups lukewarm water to wake up the yeast. Before breakfast, reserve 1 cup of starter in the crock and store in a cool place for the next batch. Add to your batter:

2 eggs
½ tsp salt
1 tbl sugar or maple syrup
1 tsp baking soda
1 tsp lukewarm water
2 tbl liquid shortening

Pour by spoonfuls onto a hot (but not smoking) griddle. Sprinkle batter with fresh blueberries. Turn cakes when bubbles appear and the underside is golden brown.

HAWAII

by REEVE L. BROWN

Of all the states in the Union, there is only one we call "paradise"—Hawaii. It is an unearthly, improbable Eden, consisting of a chain of volcanic islands scattered in the Pacific Ocean more than 2,000 miles from the American mainland.

Hawaii's benign climate, lush vegetation and spectacular landscapes have long provided a haven for travelers, from the ancient Polynesians migrating northeast across the vast Pacific to today's tourist who steps off a jet airplane.

Human beings have not been the only visitors to the islands. Dolphins as well as surfers play in the swelling waves near white sand beaches. Humpback whales breach, their spouts appearing like puffs of smoke between shoreline and horizon. And below these warm waters lies a world of dreams, where a diver can float through enchanted gardens of feathery hydroid colonies and the beckoning castles and caverns of coral reefs. Moving with him—now in light, now in shadow—are multitudes of brilliantly colored fish: parrots, angels, butterflies. Here, too, Hawaiian fishermen may set their nets for *akule* (mackerel) which sometimes come inside the reefs. Game fishermen go beyond the reef to try for tuna, marlin, wahoo and *mahimahi* (dolphin fish).

The Hawaiian experience is a total immersion in light, color and fragrance. Flowers are everywhere. They hang in colorful garlands in the lei-sellers' stalls near Waikiki, on Oahu. They flourish beside every road and stream. They run wild near the breathtaking waterfalls along the Molokai cliffs and in the rain-drenched forests of Maui and Kauai.

Many of Hawaii's flowering plants are not true natives. From the time of the early

Surfers watching the sun set on calm Manunalua
Bay hope for better waves to ride tomorrow.
(Overleaf) Pristine Lumahai Beach on Kauai
could satisfy anyone's dream of paradise.

Hawaii is a natural greenhouse for lush, exotic plants like (left to right) orchids, anthuriums and plumeria.

Polynesians, travelers have brought exotic flowers with them. Among the more extraordinary are the broad-leaved, long-stemmed anthuriums, whose garish flat spathes shelter tiny cylindrical clusters of delicate flowers, and the plumeria with its stout, stubby branches and strong-scented petals.

Besides anthuriums and plumeria, carnations, jasmine, yellow ginger, gardenias and vanda orchids are fashioned into leis. Each flower lends its own significance to the wreaths, which traditionally express sentiments for specific occasions.

Loke-lani (roses) may celebrate a baby's christening. Carnations are favorites at high school graduations, and Hawaiian brides often carry *pikake* (jasmine). Garlands of maile leaves—oval-pointed leaves that look like bay leaves—appear at every celebration.

Hawaii's geographical isolation has fostered the evolution of a number of unusual birds, whose ancestors landed here and were then separated for thousands of years from their mainland counterparts. Unfortunately, many of these uniquely Hawaiian birds have become extinct, and others are threatened by loss of habitat and by competition from more recently imported species, such as the Chinese thrush and the Japanese bush warbler brought in by immigrants in the early 1900's, as well as the ubiquitous Myna bird, a native of southeast Asia. Still, in the tangled, rugged interior of

177

The dense, misty wilds of Kauai evoke
primeval scenes the ancestors of the
nene goose probably found when landing
on Hawaii thousands of years ago.

Kauai, in the rain forests of Kilauea, on the
"Big Island" of Hawaii, and on the wet northeastern slopes of Haleakala Crater, on Maui,
some native species can still be seen. The red
of the *apapane* and the green of the *amakihi,*
two of the remaining Hawaiian honeycreepers,
flash as these birds probe the wild garden
for nectar and insects.

    Hawaii's state bird, the nene goose, is now
making a comeback from near extinction.
Mongooses and other mammals had endangered
this ground nester by devouring its eggs and
goslings. Man, too, played a part by hunting the
nene excessively and moving into its habitat.

    The state's only native mammals are the
Hawaiian bat and the monk seal. The bats still

Clear water, colorful catamarans and playful dolphins heighten the excitement of living on America's tropical island state.

(Overleaf) Sooty terns soar over Hawaii when it's breeding time.

thrive on the island of Hawaii, but the monk seals need the protection of the Hawaiian Islands National Wildlife Refuge in the Northwestern Hawaiian Islands (or Leeward Islands). This park also serves as a sanctuary for millions of seabirds, including Laysan albatrosses returning just to breed after soaring for months over the ocean and blue-faced boobies roosting in shallow nests on sandy cliff tops.

As you sail in Hawaiian waters today you may find bottlenose dolphins, playful and unafraid, leaping in the wake of your boat. Or while strolling down a beach you may see overhead a huge flock of sooty terns startled into flight by some intrusion into their nesting area. On a flight from Honolulu to the outer islands, your pilot may dip a wing to point out a breaching humpback whale, flukes in the air and spray flying. Whether it's whales, waterfalls, orchids or volcanoes you seek, you'll find them on these islands, for here the exotic and the fantastic have become commonplace, making Hawaii for all who live and travel here a paradise on earth.

HAWAIIAN
ALMANAC

THE ALOHA STATE

Polynesians named Hawaii for their homeland, *Havaiki*.

DRESSED TO THE TEETH

The sperm whale, once plentiful in Hawaiian waters, was hunted in the 19th century mainly for its valuable oil, but island craftsmen found the whale's teeth a perfect medium for carving jewelry. The four- to five-inch conical teeth, polished to a high gloss, hung from handsome necklaces and bracelets. Both men and women wore the *lei Palaola* (whale's tooth necklace) for religious purposes, and hula dancers decorated their ceremonial costumes with the jewelry.

UNWIELDY WILIWILIS

Surfing originated in Hawaii long ago and was enjoyed by nobility and common folk alike. The chiefs rode on special boards called *wiliwilis*. Made out of koa

wood rubbed with coconut oil, these boards were narrow, up to eighteen feet long and weighed a hefty one hundred fifty pounds. Both the top and bottom were convex, making them unstable as well as cumbersome. The boards were so unwieldy that riders had to take the waves lying down.

THE LONG AND SHORT OF IT

In Hawaiian, a tiny reef fish is called *humuhumunukunukuapua'a* and a giant ocean fish is called *a'u*.

LET IT SNOW

Tropical islands do have snow. Mauna Loa (13,680 ft.), Mauna Kea (13,784 ft.) and Haleakala (10,023 ft.)—three of Hawaii's highest mountains—may be capped with a foot or more of snow several times a year. Snow occasionally falls at elevations as low as 7,000 feet, but it quickly

melts there, as temperatures seldom dip below the freezing point even at 11,000 feet.

TRADE WINDS

All through the night
and all day long
I hear the croon
of the trade-wind's song
Played on the harp
of the palm tree's fronds,
A song for the hearts
of vagabonds.

— Don Blanding

TREASURE TROVE

While lolling on the white sand beaches at Diamond Head, you may notice jewel-like patches of brilliant green sand. The "jewels" were created by waves that ground up rocks containing the mineral olivine. The more olivine in the rocks, the more intense the color.

ROYAL BIRD

The oo, a species of honeyeater, was called "royal bird" because Hawaiian chiefs donned shimmering golden-yellow cloaks made of oo feathers. King Kamehameha's elegant ceremonial cloak contained about 80,000 plumes.

Originally, hunters killed thousands of the birds, as each oo had only two of these coveted yellow feathers. When hunting began to endanger the species, the chiefs commanded that the birds be trapped and then released after the feathers were removed. Still, the population had declined dangerously, and later habitat destruction resulted in the extinction of the oo.

THE ICEMAN COMETH BY SHIP

Before refrigeration came to Hawaii, an enterprising businessman in Honolulu imported blocks of ice from New England. Packed in sawdust, the blocks arrived by sailing ship via Cape Horn. The ice was stored in a wooden ice house that had double walls insulated with charcoal. The ice sold for 25¢ a pound in 1858 and for only 5¢ a pound in 1859, the year of the last shipment.

DUST JUMPING

Many of us remember the joys of childhood leaf-raking when we'd take turns jumping into piles of dried leaves. Centuries ago in Hawaii, the Kau natives on the main island enjoyed a similar sport—dust jumping. Deposits of the dust—fine volcanic ash—were several feet deep in some places. The game was to jump off high banks and *plop* softly into the dust.

PINEAPPLE BOUQUET

The pineapple plant flowers as a lavender bouquet. After the petals fall, tiny fruits slowly fuse into one large one.

MELE KALIKIMAKA

Mele Kalikimaka—Merry Christmas—has been a traditional seasonal greeting in Hawaii ever since the Christian missionaries arrived on the islands a hundred and forty years ago. To celebrate this festive season, Hawaiians hang strings of lights on fir trees imported from California and Washington or on native pine, cypress or macadamia nut trees. Ti leaf or Oregon holly wreaths are a common sight. Island cooks may prepare a mainland Christmas dinner of turkey, cranberry sauce and plum pudding or may choose Peking duck, Philippine suckling pig or Japanese tempura. Dessert may include macadamia nut brittle.

MACADAMIA NUT BRITTLE

2 tbl butter
2 cups sugar
1 cup white corn syrup
2 tsp baking soda
1½ cups chopped
   macadamia nuts
½ cup water

With 1 tbl of butter, grease baking sheet. Combine sugar, corn syrup and water and cook slowly 'til syrup reaches hard-crack stage, 300°. Remove from heat. Stir in 1 tbl butter, soda and nuts. Pour a thin layer of the mixture on baking sheet. When cold, break into pieces.

ALASKA

by BOYD NORTON

In describing Alaska you find your stock of adjectives sadly deficient and quickly depleted. Quite simply, Alaska is the quintessence of wilderness, wildlife and grand scenery in America. Mere mention of this state brings about a curious change in people. Eyes become glazed with that faraway look. "Alaska," the word is whispered with quiet reverence. "I'd like to go there sometime."

One of the first things you discover about Alaska is a different idea of travel. Here a plane may replace the station wagon. Come weekends, the family hops into a Cessna, not a Chevy, for that fishing, hunting or camping trip—often hundreds of miles from home. The reason for this winged travel is obvious: the vastness, ruggedness and wildness of our 49th state. Most of Alaska is roadless, and considering the damage bulldozers wreak on such fragile eco-

systems, that's just as well. The state's more than seven thousand registered planes make its wild country accessible without having to build a maze of highways.

For many Alaskans, the airplane is the only link between wilderness homes and the outside world. Chuck and Sara Hornberger's place is on Lake Clark at the edge of the new Lake Clark National Park, one hundred and fifty air miles southwest of Anchorage. Despite its harsh climate (25 to 30 below zero for weeks on end in winter), this land sustains them well. Moose and caribou are plentiful, and in summer Sara's garden explodes during the 18 to 21 hours of sunlight to provide a bountiful harvest of beans, cucumbers, lettuce—even strawberries.

Alaska is a land of extremes. At the Kobuk sand dunes, 25 miles north of the Arctic Circle, summertime temperatures can hit 100 degrees.

This pocket of civilization on Lake Clark punctuates the vastness of the Alaskan landscape. (Overleaf) Floatplanes ferry sportsmen and vacationing families into Alaska's remote Tikchik Lake.

188

A hiker trekking on tundra may see powerful brown bears, gentle willow ptarmigan or majestic caribou.

In winter the mercury here can plunge to 70 below. The wildlife is finely tuned to such wild seasonal swings. Great brown bears on the Alaska Peninsula escape winter's bitterness and lack of food by denning up. Caribou survive by roaming long distances over the vast tundra. In herds numbering many thousands, these restless arctic deer migrate each year from summer to winter feeding grounds, lest they overgraze the life-giving lichens. For the willow ptarmigan, the state bird, winter dictates a change in plumage —from mottled brown to a dazzling snow

"It's an oogli," Eskimos say of this
strand of beach on Round Island peninsula where walruses flop to sleep and sun.

white that makes these northern relatives of the
grouse virtually disappear.

With a coastline longer than that of the
entire lower 48 states, it's not surprising that
Alaska enjoys the riches of the sea. It was the
abundance of seals and walruses that allowed
early Eskimo cultures to flourish, some nearly as
far back as the end of the last ice age over
9,000 years ago.

Because of their size (adult males weigh
nearly a ton), walruses were a bountiful source
of food and fuel. Rendered fat produced oil for

lamps and cooking. And those ivory tusks—some over three feet long—were prized by native carvers. Eskimos still hunt the walrus; but in northeast Bristol Bay, islands have been set aside as sanctuaries. Now the walrus population is rapidly increasing after decades of decline.

To some people making their first journey to the state, it's a rude shock to find it's not all wilderness. Anchorage is a big modern city with skyscrapers, fine restaurants and even traffic jams. But over most of the state, the only touch of civilization may be a lonely outpost that

Cooper's Landing Store is to neighbors what cottonwood trees are to these bald eagles on the Chilkat River—a great place to congregate on a winter's afternoon.

194

Dall sheep ewes and lambs winter on lower slopes where wind uncovers grasses.

serves as post office, general store, social center and ultimate source of news and gossip for those who live in wilderness isolation. Beans, bacon, garden seeds, fish hooks, rifles or new parts for your plane; just place your order and eventually it will arrive by air or boat or possibly even dogsled. Not many Alaskans would trade away this lack of "civilization." For one thing, it allows wildlife to thrive. Even the bald eagle and the timber wolf—both endangered in most of the rest of the United States—flourish in this land spared of too many people.

196

You can't travel far in Alaska without seeing or feeling the presence of Mt. McKinley. In a state already crammed chock-full of breath-taking scenery, this mountain—called *Denali,* the "High One," by early natives—is literally the icing on it all. Its 20,320 feet make it North America's highest peak. Not even the famed and lofty Himalayas rise so abruptly above their surroundings as does this overwhelming mountain: it sweeps upward from the land in a bold vertical rise of more than 18,900 feet. But even when the High One is shrouded in clouds and lost to view, Denali National Park is worth the visit. The hills at the foot of McKinley roll away to a seemingly endless wilderness. The icy rivers, fed by Denali's glaciers, run together in lazy *S* patterns as they flow through creases in the land. On a hillside a grizzly and her two cubs browse among the blueberry bushes, their fur glowing in the morning sunlight. Higher on that hillside a band of Dall sheep grazes unconcerned. Stark white, these relatives of the Rocky Mountain bighorn may allow you to approach within fifty feet. But as you

raise the field glasses for another look, something below catches your attention. Out of a willow thicket a bull moose, regal with his five-foot-wide antlers, ambles toward you. Down the road and around the next hillside it may be a small band of caribou that grabs your attention, grazing in their usual restive way and obviously not worried by your presence. Perhaps in no other part of the state can you experience Alaska—its land and its wildlife—in such a concentration. It is a little like seeing the world when it was young: raw, rugged, untouched.

Salmon fishing means work, for the commercial operator hauling his nets and for the native drying his catch for winter.

At times it almost seems as though Alaska was created on purpose to please everyone who loves the out-of-doors. A downeast Maine fisherman will feel at home. Instead of lobster, however, it is salmon or king crab that he hauls in by net or trap. And as in New England, there are deep-rooted traditions. Here those roots may be thousands of years old: native fishermen may still dry their salmon on wooden racks in the way of their ancestors. And in some Eskimo villages, the traps used in winter to fish through holes in frozen rivers are painstakingly woven

from reeds and willow branches, as they have been for centuries.

"Tell me about Alaska," a friend asks. But what can you say? How do you describe the overpowering sense of space and freedom. What can you say about the special quality of light, the interplay of cloud and sky, the glacier-draped mountains that defy simple words. Is it possible to convey to someone the impact of this place on the senses, from the rich, earthy smell of tundra to the profound silence? How do you relate the quickening of the pulse at the sight of a polar bear loping along, white fur shimmering in the sunlight, or of a snowy owl as it swoops silently down to its tundra nest? How on earth do you describe it all?

You can't, of course, and there's little point in trying. So you smile, mumble a few platitudes sprinkled with words like "big" and "beautiful" and let it go at that. But all the while you're thinking about the next time, perhaps a longer visit to explore that hidden valley in the Brooks Range, make that canoe trip down the Noatak, visit the Wrangell Mountains, see the Kenai Fjords, fish in Iliamna Lake . . .

The snowy owl will soon return to his mate and chicks with a lemming or rabbit plucked from the arctic tundra.

ALASKAN
ALMANAC

THE LAST FRONTIER

Our fiftieth state, Alaska, derives its name from the Aleut word *a-la-as-ka*, which means "the great country."

WALRUS VAGABONDS

When walruses migrate through the Bering Strait, they sometimes prefer to do it the easy way. Although good swimmers, they like to haul themselves onto blocks of floating ice going their way and hitch a free ride. When swimming in calm seas, they may rest by taking naps. They inflate large air sacs in their necks and doze as they bob up and down like buoys.

Some walruses do not complete the migration, as Eskimos still hunt these animals in the spring and fall. Alaskan natives learned centuries ago to use walrus skin, organs and bones to make everything from rope to musical instruments to window panes.

WILDLIFE SIGNS

The carved totem poles and the calendar of the Tlingit Indians of coastal Alaska reveal how important wildlife was to them in their daily lives.

March: *Heen-tahn-nough-kee-ahnie-dis*—when seaweed begins growth
July: *Ut-gut-du-dis*—when young seals are born
September: *Dis-yutty*—when young animals are matured
November: *Koch-waha-dis*—when bear are denning up

TAKING OUT THE BITE

The number of mosquitos per cubic foot in Alaska is among the highest in the world. A good way to stop the itch of bites is to wet the skin and sprinkle on meat tenderizer. The tenderizer breaks down the injected protein which causes the discomfort.

But why get bitten at all, when it's so easy to avoid? The rules are few and simple: wear light colors (mosquitos love dark ones), go outside only on breezy, sunny days (the beasts attack more frequently in still air), and avoid breathing—mosquitos home in on exhaled carbon dioxide!

THE IDITAROD

Each year some fifty dog sled teams struggle over 1200 miles of rugged arctic terrain from Anchorage to Nome. The two- to four-week trip is a grueling test of stamina. For the dogs, it is a physical challenge to strain against the 200-pound sled in the energy-sapping cold. For the mushers (drivers), it is even more demanding. They must see to their dogs, pampering them with hot meals prepared according to secret recipes, tying on sealskin booties that protect paws from jagged ice, and getting the required veterinary exam at each checkpoint. The musher must also calculate the pace, choose a lead dog and even keep the team from chasing moose or caribou.

SIX FEET OF CRAB

The king crab is the biggest crab found in Alaskan waters. The largest adults may weigh up to twenty pounds and have a leg span of six feet. Meat from a single leg of these crabs makes a mighty feast.

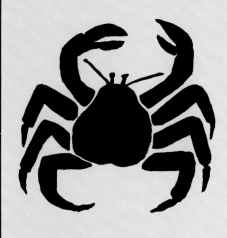

PAMPERING BABY

Early Eskimos invented an ingenious diaper. On display in the Alaska State Museum in Juneau is a diaper made of white fawn skin edged in fur and lined with dried moss that could be replaced as needed. A version of today's disposable diaper!

BEARS HAVE BAD TEMPERS, TOO

When a polar bear misses its catch, its temper sometimes shows. One grouchy polar bear that just missed a seal meal hurled pieces of ice into the sea. Another bear slapped and splashed the water again and again, and still another gave out an explosive roar and tossed snow high into the air.

WINTER'S NIGHT CASSEROLE

Cabbages can grow to giant sizes in the Matanuska Valley. Nineteen hours of sunlight for the 120-day growing season have created specimens weighing up to 70 pounds. Hunters too can claim a good harvest, for large game abound in Alaska. Gardeners, hunters and gourmets everywhere can enjoy this savory winter's night casserole.

1 cabbage (8-10 in.)
1 pound ground venison—moose, elk, caribou or deer—(or substitute beef or veal)
½ pound of hot sausage
2 tbl each of parsley and dill
1 egg
1 small onion, minced
1 clove garlic, chopped
1 cup beef stock
6 ounces tomato paste
6-8 mushrooms
1 cup cooked rice
Salt and pepper

Cook the cabbage in boiling water for 10 min. Drain. Scoop out center. Mix meat, sausage, egg, onion, garlic, rice and parsley. Season. Fill the center with the mixture. Tie the cabbage with string. Place in casserole with the stock, tomato paste, mushrooms and dill. Bake covered at 300° for 1½ hours.

INDEX TO PHOTOS

CREDITS

PICTURES

Illustrations by Susan Foster

Cover: Douglas Cross.
Page 1: Gary R. Zahm. 2-3:
Jim Brandenburg. 4: Clyde H. Smith.

THE NORTHEAST
Pages 6-7: Gene Ahrens/Bruce
Coleman, Inc. 9: Richard W.
Brown. 10: Brian Milne. 10-11:
Richard W. Brown. 11: John
Ebeling. 12: Richard W. Brown.
13 Left: Larry West; right: Robert
O. Joslin. 14: Wayne Lankinen/
Valan Photos. 14-15: Richard W.
Brown. 16-17: Clyde H. Smith.
18-19: Richard W. Brown. 20-21:
Larry Ditto. 22: Robert P. Carr.
22-23: Richard W. Brown. 24-25:
DeWitt Jones/Woodfin Camp, Inc.
25: Leonard Lee Rue III/Animals
Animals. 26: Helen Rhode. 27:
Annie Griffiths. 28-29: Dwight R.

Kuhn. 29: Dr. G. J. Chafaris. 30:
George H. Harrison. 30-31: Clyde
H. Smith. 31: Douglas Faulkner/
Sally Faulkner Collection. 32-33:
Richard W. Brown. 34-35: Richard
W. Brown. 36-37: Grant Heilman/
Grant Heilman Photography.

THE SOUTH
Pages 40-41: Ken Lewis/Earth
Scenes. 43: Zig Leszczynski/Earth
Scenes. 44: Larry West. 45: Joe
McDonald. 46 Top: Breck P. Kent;
bottom: Sonja Bullaty and Angelo
Lomeo ©. 47: Larry West. 48:
Breck P. Kent/Animals Animals.
49: John Trott. 50: Jerry Smith.
50-51: Hans Reinhard/Bruce
Coleman, Inc. 52-53: Anderson/
FPG. 53: David Cavagnaro.
54-55: James H. Carmichael, Jr.
56-57: C. C. Lockwood/Earth
Scenes. 58: John Shaw. 59: Wendell
D. Metzen. 60: Jeff Foott. 61:
Thase Daniel. 62: James H.
Carmichael, Jr./Bruce Coleman,
Inc. 63: Wendell D. Metzen.

THE MIDWEST
Pages 66-67: Jim Brandenburg. 69:
Robert P. Carr. 70-71: Ken
Dequaine. 72-73: John Ebeling.
74-75: Larry Ditto. 76: George H.
Harrison. 77: John Ebeling. 78:
Stephen J. Krasemann/DRK Photo.
79: Jim Brandenburg. 80: Grant
Heilman/Grant Heilman
Photography. 81: W. Perry
Conway/Grant Heilman
Photography. 82-83: David
Muench. 84 Top: George H.
Harrison. 84-85: Everett C.
Johnson. 86: Alvin E. Staffan. 87:
Robert P. Carr/Bruce Coleman, Inc.
88: R. L. Kothenbeutel. 89:
Everett C. Johnson.

MOUNTAIN STATES
Pages 92-93: Kent & Donna
Dannen. 95: Russell Lamb. 96:
Jean-Marie Jro/Valan Photos. 97:
Larry Ditto. 98-99: Gary N. Hill.
99: Charles M. Howe/Animals
Animals. 100-101: Michael S.
Quinton. 102-103: © Douglas
Faulkner. 103: John Ebeling. 104:
Thase Daniel. 105 Top: Jen & Des
Bartlett/Bruce Coleman, Inc.;
bottom: Neal & Mary Jane Mishler.
106: Kent & Donna Dannen. 107:
Stephen J. Krasemann/DRK Photo.
108: Thase Daniel. 109 Top: Jeff
Foott; bottom: Wayne Lankinen/
Valan Photos. 110-111: Buddy
Mays. 112: Patti Murray/Animals
Animals. 113: Tim Kelly/Black
Star. 114-115: Bill McRae. 116:
Tom & Pat Leeson. 117: Kent &
Donna Dannen. 118-119: Tom &
Pat Leeson.

THE SOUTHWEST
Pages 122-123: Robert P. Carr.
125: Alan Pitcairn/Grant Heilman
Photography. 126: Chuck O'Rear/
Woodfin Camp, Inc. 127: Jen &
Des Bartlett/Bruce Coleman, Inc.
128 Top: David Cavagnaro;
bottom: Ernest Wilkinson/Animals
Animals. 129: John Shaw. 130
Top: Cosmos Blank/National
Audubon Society Collection/
Photo Researchers, Inc.; bottom:
Grace A. Thompson. 131: Zig
Leszczynski/Animals Animals.
132: John Blaustein. 132-133:
Charles G. Summers, Jr. 133: J. C.
Stevenson/Animals Animals.
134-135: David Muench.
136-137: Gary R. Zahm. 138:
Leonard Lee Rue III. 139: Wyman
P. Meinzer, Jr. 140: Robert P.
Carr. 141 Top: Robert P. Carr;
bottom: C. Allan Morgan.

PACIFIC STATES

Pages 144-145: Ray Atkeson. 147: Ken Balcomb. 148-149: Jeff Foott/Bruce Coleman, Inc. 149: Jeff Foott. 150-151: Tupper Ansel Blake. 152: E. R. Degginger/Earth Scenes. 153: David Cavagnaro. 154-155: Edison Ryals. 156-157: Robert Y. Kaufman/YOGI. 158 Top left: Norman Owen Tomalin/Bruce Coleman, Inc.; bottom right: David F. Robinson. 159: Craig Aurness/Woodfin Camp, Inc. 160: C. Allan Morgan. 161: Chuck Place. 162-163: Gary R. Zahm. 163: Jim Anderson. 164: Gene Ahrens. 165 Left: Tom & Pat Leeson; right: Art Wolf. 166: Keith Gunnar. 167: David Muench. 168-169: Tom & Pat Leeson.

HAWAII

Pages 172-173: Gene Ahrens. 175: Craig Aurness/Woodfin Camp, Inc. 176: Mark S. Carlson. 176-177: David Cavagnaro. 177: Werner Stoy/Camera Hawaii/Bruce Coleman, Inc. 178: George H. Harrison. 178-179: David Muench. 180: Stephen J. Krasemann/DRK Photo. 181: Art Wolfe. 182-183: David Cavagnaro.

ALASKA

Pages 186-187: Erwin & Peggy Bauer. 189: Jim Brandenburg. 190 Top: Steven C. Kaufman; bottom: Bill Byrne. 191: Steven C. Kaufman. 192: Stephen J. Krasemann/DRK Photo. 193: Fred Bruemmer. 194: Helen Rhode. 195: Martin W. Grosnick. 196-197: Mark Newman/Animals Animals. 198 Top: Steve McCutcheon; bottom: Steven C. Wilson. 199: Tony Dawson. 200-201: Stephen Maslowski.

TEXT

The Editors wish to thank the persons and publishers listed below for permission to include in our book the following poems:

"Counting-Out Rhyme" (page 38), by Edna St. Vincent Millay from *Collected Poems,* Harper & Row. Copyright 1928, 1955 by Edna St. Vincent Millay and Norma Millay Ellis.

"Out Where The West Begins" (page 121), from *Out Where the West Begins* and Other Small Songs of a Big Country by Arthur Chapman. Copyright 1916, 1917 by Arthur Chapman. Copyright renewed 1945 by Kathleen C. Chapman. Reprinted by permission of Houghton Mifflin Company.

"Trade Winds" (page 184), from *Pictures of Paradise* by Don Blanding; Dodd, Mead and Company, Inc., publishers.

Library of Congress
Cataloging in
Publication Data

Main entry under title:

America's wildlife sampler.

Includes index.
1. Natural history—United States—Addresses, essays, lectures.
2. Zoology—United States—Addresses, essays, lectures.
I. National Wildlife Federation
QH104.A75   1982   591.973
ISBN O-912186-45-3   82-60674

NATIONAL WILDLIFE FEDERATION

1412 16th Street, N.W.
Washington, D.C. 20036

Dr. Jay D. Hair
Executive Vice President

James D. Davis
Senior Vice President
Membership Development
and Publications

STAFF FOR THIS BOOK

Howard F. Robinson
Managing Editor

Barbara Peters
Editor

Donna Miller
Design Director

Polly S. White
Art Editor

Michael E. Loomis
Assistant Art Editor

Laura B. Ackerman
Research Editor

Dr. Raymond E. Johnson
Wildlife Consultant

Vi Kirksey
Editorial Assistant

Priscilla Sharpless
Production and Printing

Carol Kaufman
Production Artist

Margaret E. Wolf
Permissions Editor

ACKNOWLEDGMENTS

To capture the spirit of each region of our country and, at the same time, to be accurate in every detail, we needed generous help from knowledgeable people all across America. We are especially grateful to the following individuals:

Dr. Edward E.C. Clebsch, Department of Botany, and Dr. Paul A. Delcourt, Department of Geology, University of Tennessee; Dr. John J. Fay and Mr. Jay M. Sheppard, U.S. Department of the Interior, Office of Endangered Species; and the staff of the Mammal Division, Smithsonian Institution.

We also want to thank the following NWF staff for their constant cooperation: April Bohannan, Assistant Librarian; Dr. S. Douglas Miller and his staff, NWF Institute for Wildlife Research; Dr. Albert A. Clark, NWF Southern Wetlands Project; Mr. Craig Tufts, Education Center Programs; and the editors of *National Wildlife* and *International Wildlife* and of *Ranger Rick's Nature Magazine*.